SCARS IN THE MEMORY

SCARS IN THE MEMORY

Editorial Capitán San Luis
Havana, 2006

Original title in Spanish: *Cicatrices en la memoria* / Editorial advisor: Eduardo Heras León / Design interior: Rafael Morante Boyerizo / Cover Design: Eugenio Sagues / Production: Julio A. Cubría Vichot / Photography: Roberto Chávez Miranda / Translation: Ana V. Portela

ISBN: 959-211-285-1

Editorial Capitán San Luis, Ave. 25 no. 3406, entre 34 y 36, Playa, La Habana, Cuba

roberto fernández retamar

PREFACE The monstrous attacks of September 11, 2001, that cut down the World Trade Center towers in New York and destroyed a wing of the Pentagon in Washington provoked a huge and justified rejection of the world against these horrible acts of terrorism. Cuba was one of the first countries to condemn the action and offer aid to the aggrieved people of the United States to whom we are strongly bound, in spite of the well-known political differences. Also, Cuba knows what it is all about because it has suffered numerous terrorist attacks in its own soil since 1959 in general encouraged, with rare exceptions such as the Carter government, by successive United States administrations.

There is no good or bad terrorism: all terrorism is reprehensible; nor are only the powerful who suffer when terrorism turns against them. But the mass media (often of mass disinformation) in hands of the latter spread to the four corners of the world echoes of their pain, and silence or minimize those against the poor humanity. This book aims to demonstrate how writers, living in Cuba, have recreated some of the many aggressions suffered by the country in over forty years. It is necessary to listen to their voice at a time when they intend to convince that not only the crimes of that September 11 are worthy of repudiation: attempting to erase from memory another September 11, that of 1973, when, following instructions of the current United States government at the time, La Moneda Palace in Chile was bombed causing the death of President Salvador Allende and setting up a fierce military tyranny that killed thousands of people. The Costa Gavras film of 1982, Missing *denounced the event basing its story on a young journalist from the United States who is murdered and sought by his father, memorably played by Jack Lemmon.*

Terrorist acts committed against Cuba have varied in kind and include sabotages, such as the bomb explosions in the French ship, La Coubre, on March 4, 1960 when Belgian munitions were being unloaded, munitions necessary to defend the island, or the blowing up of a Cuban civilian flight taking off from Barbados on October 6, 1976: the intellectual authors of this crime are the well known terrorists trained by the CIA Orlando Bosch, who strolls freely along the streets of Miami and Luis Posada Carriles, pardoned by the Panamanian president, Mireya Moscoso, who was planning to assassinate Fidel together with an undetermined number of students; acts of arson such as the destruction of the most important Cuban store, El Encanto, on April 13, 1961; acts of kidnapping (such as the kidnappings of the Cuban fishermen on high seas in the sixties and seventies or the famous boy, Elian, during 1999 to 2000; or planned attacks, such as the many to assassinate Fidel and other high officials or the murder of a Cuban diplomat in Portugal on April 22, 1976; the infiltration of terrorists such as the one in Caibarién on October 15, 1994; planting of bombs, as recently as September 4, 1997, that exploded in the Copacabana, Triton and Chateau Miramar hotels in Havana and the restaurant, La Bodeguita del Medio: several of these explosives were planted by a Salvadoran contracted by Posada Carriles; machine gunning from the sea, biological warfare and, of course, the well known mercenary invasion in the style of such actions in so many countries of the region: suffice the example of Guatemala in 1954. The difference lies in that the one attempted against Cuba in April of 1961 was crushed in sixty-six hours. Due to that defeat, the main US authorities set up the sinister Plan Mongoose that entailed many aggressions against Cuba and could have led to a direct attack of the Island by the United States in 1962,

6

(See Jacinto Valdés Dapena in his book Operation Mongoose: Prelude of a direct invasion on Cuba, *Havana by the Editorial Capitan San Luis, 2004).* *To dissuade the leaders of that country not to attack it and, above all, in solidarity with the socialist bloc, Cuba agreed to the Soviet suggestion of positioning atomic warhead rockets in its territory that led to the October Crisis, 1962, the most critical moment of the Cold War that put humanity on the brink of extinction. At the time of the writing of this book, there is an «International Conference:* October Crisis, a political view 40 years later» *in progress with the participation of several of the surviving protagonists of this world–shattering event: a Conference that has been characterized by sobriety and respect. That is what will happen, sooner or later, in the future events will be added to those reported in this book. These actions have cost Cuba 3 478 deaths and 2 099 disabled victims (see* Demanda del pueblo de Cuba al gobierno de los Estados Unidos por daños humanos *[presented to the Popular Provincial Court of Havana, May 31, 1999], Havana, Oficina de Publicaciones del Consejo de Estado, 1999).*

The texts that appear in this volume are examples of what Mario Benedetti called, in a useful book, Letras de emergencia *(Buenos Aires, Editorial Alfa Argentina, 1973). Several of these, for their basic quality, will by far exceed the moment that promoted its publication.*

But, undoubtedly, emphasis has been placed on these situations. And its common purpose is not only to exhibit these events but to call attention as to how Cuba has been forced to defend itself from the terrorism it has suffered, not in a lone and bitter day of September but during over forty years. A unique example of this defense was demonstrated by the five Cuban patriots who are imprisoned today in United States jails having received incredible sentences for the alleged crime of having infiltrated minor factions in Florida, mostly in Miami, that have planned terrorist actions against Cuba with the tolerance of the authorities of that nation. It is not a crime but a sign of glory to defend your country against terrorism. If, in the same manner, had the aggressor groups of September 11, 2001, that, surprisingly, were trained in the United States, been infiltrated the horrors of that day would not have to be lamented. God knows how many evils these compatriots prevented, not only for Cuba. For this reason, they have been granted the highest honor: the title of Heroes. In the epilogue of this book, Ricardo

Alarcón, President of the National Assembly of Popular Power, explains the vicissitudes of this case.

The objective of these pages is to reach the intelligence and the heart of other peoples, particularly of the United States. When Elian was kidnapped eighty percent of the US public opinion supported the return of the child to his real family and his real home. We must not be misguided by the deceit of unscrupulous leaders and confuse the noble feelings of a people that, in the 18th century began their independence revolution in America, a country that in the 19th century abolished slavery and that, in the 20th century fought nazi fascism abroad and McCarthyism within its borders. We have faith in this people, Lincoln's homeland. These pages were written, in part, thinking of him. We are sure it has not been in vain.

Havana, October 13, 2002.

eduardo   heras   león

For Nelson Heras and Enrique Ávila Guerrero,
the Old Guard

STILL LIFE At midday the factory workshops were a hive of activity drowning in a tide of heat and sweat. As we finished lunch every man fled to his corner of shade, his portion of the blessed wind, to rest out the all too brief break.

I left the canteen stuffed full and climbed the steps towards the foundry. I'd hardly crossed the threshold of the casting room when the noise of the pistons crashed onto my ears and numbed them. "I'll never get used to this infernal racket", I thought. I almost ran across the open floor, skirting the dump. They had just finished tapping the molten metal and the casts sat and smoked, contaminating the putrid air further still. In that damned place I'd found a place where sun and silence reigned and a huge whole in the breezeblock wall let the wind come dancing in. A strange oasis, perhaps, in the midst of that maelstrom of noise and dust and heat.

Then I saw him.

He had his back to me, a welder's mask in his hand. He was a tall, slight, black man. His silhouette, caught in the frame of light from the back door of the workshop, was somehow familiar. Something, some cog inside my mind began to turn and take me back, back in time. I stopped suddenly when he turned. He stared hard at me, serious at first, with his face' screwed tight. Then the grimace relaxed and a broad smile brought out the unmistakable face of a boy that came running towards me over the ripples of my memory.

- I know you from somewhere- he said - From...? From...? Wait a minute. From...?
- I know you too. From the army maybe? The artillery?
- No, no, before that. - And he closed his eyes.
- University?
- No, well before that, well before...
- From school, yes, that's it, school- I said, my memory gaining pace.
- 114! - We both said together
- Scream Palace- I added laughing- You're…? You're...? Faustino! Tino!
- And you're...Little Raul, Curly!

He came up to me and patted my rebellious hair just the way he used to. We hugged, just like the two boys in our memories.

- Faustino, Jesus! Do you realize how long it's been? It must be 20 years, pal. 20 years and look at us now! What a place for a reunion!

He pulled his mask on and cast a glance at the oven. He opened the door and stood for a few moments watching the pulsing electrodes in the heart of the chamber. He nodded to himself and banged the door shut.

- Hey, Tino, are you the duty smelter?
- Yep, I've been here a few months now.
- Weird, how come I hadn't seen you...
- Well, I've been off. Sick you know, I still am...It's my nerves.

He lowered himself onto the smelter's bench and pulled another stool from somewhere, setting it next to him.

- Come on Curly, let's catch up on old times.
- I'm glad to see you, pal.

He took the mask off and wiped the sweat from his face and neck with a grubby handkerchief.

A silence had descended on the whole foundry, as if it too was resting after lunch.

- Wow, so you're a smelter! I said - Was that what you studied? You passed your trade exams?
- No, I'm an engineer.
- An engineer? You, an engineer? Come on Tino, you were awful at math.

12

- Well, there you go. I went and got a degree and everything. From the Kiev Higher Institute of Metallurgy.

- In the USSR? Come on...you're having me on? Well, you'd better tell me the whole story - I said as I looked at him curiously.

- Not now mate, it's too long a story, and anyway...

- No, no, wait a minute. If you're an engineer, why are you working as a smelter? You should be in...Hang on, are you really an engineer?

- Of course.

- Are you sure?

I'd stood up and was looking down at him with pure disbelief. I could still remember those days in Primary School: a tall black kid as skinny as a rake, always getting into fights. Until one day, when the class bully decided to pick on me for no apparent reason, Tino suddenly came to my rescue, and was my bodyguard from that day on. He was my best friend, ever-ready for a bust-up, but we were thick as two short planks.

- Hey, are you calling me a liar?!

- No, no, course not, don't get upset. It's just that...

We fell silent. The workshop timidly found it's voice once more and the flames from the oven flickered red in a dense cloud of steam. He stood up and went to the little door once more, looking closely. Before closing it he threw in some slivers of metal and blue flames jumped up. I suddenly remembered:

- Faustino, what about Lucio?

He said nothing. He wiped the sweat from his face again, this time with a piece of burlap and lowered himself wearily down to his bench. His absent gaze penetrated the walls of the workshop, the factory. How could I forget Lucio? Faustino and Lucio, the inseparable brothers: Lucio, the elder, always protecting his brother; always looking out for him.

- What about Lucio?

- Lucio's dead, Curly - he said in a whisper.

- Dead? When?

- He died in La Coubre, March 4th, 1960.

- Was he working in the docks?

- We both were.

- But you. . .?

- I escaped by the skin of my teeth

- How?

He almost refused. I sensed his reluctance in that impatient gesture, in the quick way he lifted his hands. But something in my eyes pacified him.

- On that day it was my brigade that was unloading the ship. Lucio was on a rest day.

But I had a doctor's appointment and he stood in for me. It was his idea. When he was leaving for work I changed my mind and told him not to bother, that I could just skip a day. He just laughed. He tapped me on the chest like he always used to and said:

"You, my friend, are going to the doctor's, I'm going to work". You knew him, Curly, if he said black then black it was. You know I never argued with him. Between us two, he always had the last word. So I did what I had to do. I finished about three in the afternoon and headed back to the docks. I thought I could still sneak into the brigade that was unloading the boat. I knew they were weapons. I even caught a taxi that left me right there. When I paid I asked the driver the time "twelve past three" he told me with unusual precision. Three minutes later the boat exploded.

- Shit, Tino! You were there! What happened next? ...

- I felt a wave of heat smack me in the face and I threw myself on the floor. When I lifted my head I saw a mushroom cloud coming out of the boat. I thought it was an atomic explosion and I shit myself. Something that I thought was sweat ran down my face, but when I wiped my eyes with my sleeve I saw it was blood. I was pretty dazed and I didn't even ask myself where I was hurt. I tried to get up but dizziness caught me and everything started to spin. A siren sounded somewhere and people were running all over the place. I looked around me and saw a leg, on its own on the floor, blood and rubble everywhere. I tried to get up again. I wanted to get to the boat. But the dizziness hit me again and I fell. I've no idea how long I was down. I opened my eyes and suddenly everything was clear. I jumped up and started running. Lucio! My brother was on the boat! Lucio! But someone stopped me. Someone was pulling my shirt and screaming "you've hurt your head! Come back! It's going to blow again! Get back!" I tried to keep running but the man shoved me and I fell again. He picked me up by my shoulders and dragged me off, away from the boat.

- Did it explode again?

- Yeah, worse than the first time. Lots of people had tried to get near

14

and the second explosion killed them all. In the middle of all that chaos, I went to do what I could. I stayed there for what seemed like an eternity, still dazed, almost overpowered by the stench of gunpowder, sulphur and burnt flesh. Then the dizziness hit me stronger than ever and I almost passed out. Somebody bandaged my head. What about Lucio I was thinking? I knew that he had been on the boat, but I hoped that he'd escaped somehow. It wouldn't have been the first time. Lucio had survived a thousand knocks, had fought in the resistance against Batista, had made it through prison. No, he'd be alright. He'd get out again.

- He didn't get out, did he?

- No, Curly, he didn't. They didn't even find his body. Just a jacket he'd been wearing that day.

- And his wake?

- There was nothing to hold a wake over.

- What happened then?

- Then...nothing. The years passed. But I've never forgotten him. Lucio was everything for me. My dad, my brother, my friend. I never wanted to think of him as a martyr, he wasn't that kind of guy. He was just a regular bloke, like you or me. A man that loved life and always used to tell me "Make the most of life, Tino. There's still loads of women to bed, loads of rum to drink and loads of years to live. Keep that in your head. And never forget that one thing is sacred: work". One day, they came to our house and asked me if I would go to the Soviet Union to study. I'd only just finished High School and my grades were awful. But I was Lucio's brother, the brother of one of the martyrs of the Revolution! What was I going to say? I had to go, for him. Don't you get it? I really didn't give a shit about being an engineer or going to the USSR. I tried my best over there, even though my best was pretty bad. I thought they'd send me back to Cuba quick as a flash. But Lucio saved my bacon again. I never failed a test. No matter what I answered, I never failed. They just turned a blind eye.

- So they almost gave you your degree?

- Almost? Don't make me laugh. But they didn't give me the degree, they gave it to Lucio. He was the engineer, not me.

- What happened when you came home?

- What was always going to happen. They gave me a job here in this factory, as an engineer in Production. But after four months and about 4000 mistakes; mixing alloys, tapping, whatever, they told me to choose. Either they demoted me to smelter or they kicked me out altogether.

- So you chose smelter?

- Yeah, Curly, that's what I chose. It was the least I could do for Lucio. He'd always looked out for me, ever since we were kids. He saved my life on the day of the explosion, he made me an engineer, even though I was no good. I had to give something back, didn't I? And this time without his help. He wasn't there for me anymore, I couldn't ask his advice. So for the first time in my life I took a decision without him. It was always going to happen, sooner or later. And here I am.

- So here you are, Mr. Smelter. Well, that's just great!- I said ironically.

- Yep, Mr. Smelter.

- And you're going to stay a smelter forever?

- Yep.

- Burning your life up, rotting away in this factory?

- Yep. Just like it should be.

- What do you mean, just like it should be?

- Just that. It's my turn to suffer a little. It won't do me any harm.

- Won't do you any harm? When is it going to end? Are you going to stay here for the rest of your life?

- I don't know - he sighed - Until I've paid my dues.

- What dues, Faustino! What kind of promise is that? It's a penance, that's what it is. You're punishing yourself, can't you see?

- Alright, Curly, just leave it.

- No, I won't leave it. I was your friend once and I'm your friend now. What more can you do for Lucio? Punish yourself for not having died there with him. Can't you see you're messing up your life? Shit, mate, give yourself a break! - I shouted, angrily now.

- Leave it Curly, it's my business.

- Leave the factory, Tino.

- No, I can't

- Whatever you say you're still an engineer. You got that degree for Christ's sake!

- It's not worth the paper it's printed on.

- Of course it is - I insisted, almost begging him.

He grabbed my shoulders and stared into my face. His eyes glazed over, fading into the steam and dust that clouded the midday sun.

- Curly - and his soft voice trembled - I didn't go to the doctor that day. I went and screwed some woman, Curly. Don't you understand? He dropped me and turned away.

He raised his handkerchief to his face and wiped away the sweat. Or were they tears? He went to the oven and opened the hatch. Through the glass he watched the flames dance. Turning back he said.

- Don't worry, pal, my day is done - He pointed to the oven - I've got to watch the mix or I'll mess this one up too - he muttered, trying to smile.

He pulled his gloves off and rang the bell three times. The mix was ready. Tino walked away and was lost amidst the dust and heat of the midday workshop.

The French ship La Coubre blew up on the docks of Havana harbor. The explosion was caused by a bomb planted before the ship arrived in Cuba. This act of terrorism caused horrific damages and injuries. The bodies of 101 victims were recovered and more than 200 people were wounded.

THE CIGARETTE CASE

HIM

...she must know or she wouldn't have looked at me like that, with those eyes, like she was reading my thoughts. His hand went involuntarily to the false packet of cigarettes in his breast pocket. The woman's eyes followed his movement, just for a second, or at least he thought they did and the packet burnt into his chest and he gasped for air. He controlled his hands and flicked through the records on the shelf without taking his eyes off her for a second but she turned and was gone. *If she didn't want the record why did she ask me for it, calm down, man, calm down, nobody, not even SHE can find out about this.* He tried to concentrate on a new client that came towards him. She looked like Rosita Fornés, all blonde women looked like Rosita to him. The blonde women asked for a Lucho Gatica record, *they always want Lucho Gatica records even if they don't have dark eyes, it's like a fever.* The girl stroked the photograph on the cover, carefully tracing the singer's lips. *She'd look just like Rosita if she weren't so thin. I won't get to see the premier of the 'Merry Widow', I bet she'll be splendid, just like the paper said. Or was it sumptuous? No, splendid, as Pinelli said on television. Rosita had been into the Record Shop a few times, but she only came up to me once. I*

don't even remember what record she wanted, she was right here in front of me; I could see her lips as she spoke, her hair, it gave off sparks of heat just like I'd always imagined, and her scent, unlike any perfume somewhere between wild and delicate, or at least that's what I thought. He can't remember her voice, but he knows it wasn't like the Rosita he'd heard on television, or on the radio. He closed his eyes to remember her voice, her real voice. When he opened them Rosita was still there and she laughed in his face, he blushed and lowered his head, pretending to fill in an order form. He'd always wanted to be near her and now he wished she would go away. *I have a problem with blondes. When I was a kid I dreamt about Marilyn Monroe every night, always the same dream; I would fly into a city and there she was, looking out of the window of a tall building, she would walk to the bathroom, nude, or in a towel that sometimes looked like a coat of feathers, sometimes like a nightgown my mother used to wear that's still there at home. Every time I see it I stroke it and feel like I'm touching her skin, in the dream. Marilyn always wore lipstick and high heels, red ones, they say we don't dream in colors but those were red, bright red; the rest was in black and white, or gray, but her lips and her shoes were bright red.* When she turned towards the window and saw him he began to fall, always backwards. It was a long fall, like he was sliding down a long shaft into a sticky, transparent, endless tunnel. As he fell he no longer saw the city but rather a place near the sea, full of coconut trees; some trees swayed violently in the wind, crazy trees, other were still. When he woke, it was always morning already and he lay awake for a long time with fear in his chest and grief in his guts that pinned him to the bed. *I've got that feeling now, but it won't be long. At six o'clock the buzzer will go and people will start to leave the shop.* He knows that SHE will be one of the last, like always. *If she stays, that's her problem...* he suppressed the idea. From the minute Mario Pombo gave him "the mission" he insisted on two things: first, he'd plant the bomb on his way out so it would go off at night, when the shop was closed, and second, that all the arrangements were to be in the hands of the Americans or their people. "They've given me the bomb" Mario replied "and it's as strong as one hundred Molotov cocktails. You've just got to plant it. Don't worry about anything else". He had lost confidence in the Cubans. He didn't tell that to Pombo. Too many screw-ups. The net was drawing in, he could feel it; he couldn't even walk down the street without feeling eyes on him, burning. Just yesterday he'd hurled abuse at some old guy who looked at him. Then he'd been ashamed because the old man, with tears welling up in his eyes, had explained that he looked just like a son he'd lost many years ago; the same walk, the same hair, even the same mannerisms as the dead Carlos he still searched for when he knew it was hopeless because he'd buried him with his own hands. *That old bastard ruined my day, and my night, because I didn't sleep a wink. What a stupid fucking coincidence that the bastard was called Carlos, do I look tired?, I've washed my face three times already, and the damn clock must have stopped, will it never be six o'clock so all these people can go? Fuck! why did everyone decide to come to "El Encanto" today; take it easy kid, take it easy, stop touching the frigging records, people will get suspicious. Tomorrow all this will be ashes and you'll be long gone. I'd better be, that was the deal, that they'd get me out of here the same day, they know that, Pombo knows I'm not going to stay here, they're not going to get me like they got Eduardo and Dalmacio. They got shot because they were stupid. No, not because they were stupid, but because we're playing hardball now, and if you get caught you're going to get burnt; it's easy from the outside, or protected by Embassies, but here you've really got to have balls, real balls and guts, I'm sure SHE didn't buy that it was a pack of Edens. What an idiot, why did I take them out? It looks alright from a distance but close up you can tell it's a bomb, why the hell won't the clock hurry up, and who's she? Surely Rosita wouldn't come to the Shop at this time, why on earth did they let that blonde in, if Rosita's here I can't blow the shop up; if anything goes wrong you'll be in the slammer by tomorrow morning, even if you don't do it, you saw it in her eyes, SHE hasn't figured it out yet, but she will, she's got all night to think about it, anyway, her husband's knocking about somewhere talking shit and marching for the military and her little son is with the Russians. This is definitely Communism, nobody can fool me, that's why I'm going to blow this damn store up and then I'm out of here, it's not bloody Rosita! her nose is way too big, SHE will stay, when the time comes I'll do what I have to do, if they hadn't put that stupid little bomb outside the other day everything would be easier, the only thing that little fire cracker did was break a few windows on Galiano street, draw their attention and make my job even more difficult; never mind, come on man, you can do it. The car's out there waiting for you, they think that firecracker was the Big Attack and that nobody would dare try anything else now, but you're here right now with that bomb in your pocket, don't touch it again for Christ's sake, or do you actually want them to catch you at it? There's the buzzer, come on let's get closed up, they've already started to go and you didn't even notice, cool it man, don't get your handkerchief out again, you're not even sweating it's just nerves come on, get down to it, you know where you've got to put it, right in the middle of the clothes, almost everyone's gone, don't rush, shit! careful, that's it, right there, no-one's looking, when this goes off it's going to make a god awful mess, but you'll be long gone, stop looking about, you're a bloody lighthouse giving signals, get back to your department now; there's nothing to do there; listen to me, that's not going to go off so quick, walk nice and slow, like you were in the park,' I want to get out now; hang on, there's time, now go, softly, softly, say goodbye to them, say see you tomorrow although tomorrow none of this will be left and they'll be looking for you in every bastard nook and cranny,' that militia guard looked at me, she's following me,' no one's following you,' I bet that old bastard old man bleated, now he's coming up behind me; there's no old man behind you, it's an old woman, there's the car, go on get in, don't run for Christ's sake, don't speak to the driver, he knows where to take you; I did it I planted the bomb, it should be burning by now, no one can stop it now, and SHE must still be upstairs, I know she's up there, if she doesn't come down she's had it, that's her problem,' no that's your problem, you'll be fucked as well if she gets toasted, if they catch you they'll shoot you,' they are not going to catch me, I told them plain and simple that I wanted out tonight, tomorrow I'll read about it in the paper, that I, Carlos Gonzalez Vidal, know how to do things right. not like those dickheads who handed in their weapons and then yakked like parrots,' you want to get out because you know that if they catch you, you'll spill your guts with the first slap,' I'm no coward though! you try spending a day with a bomb in you pocket, everyone watching you and asking for cigarettes and you have to say you haven't got any, they look at the lump in your shirt pocket and you have to do the actor bit and put that face on, like it pisses you off when people ask you for a cigarette, and you wouldn't give them one if they were the last person on earth and then spend all day worrying that the guy's going to say something and they'll get suspicious and take a look in that cigarette case, that would have been best; what do you mean best? what the hell are you thinking; I did what I had to do and if SHE doesn't get out it's just fate, or whatever, this car's going so slow, why the hell is he driving all around Havana; easy, it's done, the driver's just following orders, don't look at him, don't talk to him, he can't know who you are because he's staying here, in the lion's den, he's not getting out; fuck him, I'm getting out, that was the deal and they'd better stick to it; easy kid, they're doing their part, the car was there at the right time and place, just like Mario said, here's the flashlight, remember the signals: one long, three short, two long, I've been repeating it ever since they told me, I wish I could be out of here quicker than that light, I'd better check the bulb and the batteries; don't start making the signal inside the car for Christ's sake; where's this guy taking me now, why doesn't he take me straight to Baracoa, the store will be an inferno by now. SHE must have got out, I'm sure she's out.*

HER

...don't call me again get out while there's time, I'm stuck, maybe ten minutes ago I could have forced the door to the stairs, but there's no way now, who could have done this...? SHE will never figure it out, and even if she does I'll be long gone, sitting in some bar drinking a beer, a hero. **It must have been someone from here, an employee, but who?**

Martinez? No, he's too cowardy to do this; he just talks nonsense under his breath, nothing more. She tries to move the carriages that warp in the increasing heat she wants to push those shelves down but they are too hot, the walls buckle with the heat and seem about to explode *SHE got out, please God let her get out because if she doesn't you know what you'll get, I'm sure she got out, I can almost see her now giving orders.* **Maybe it was one of the last customers, the Shop was busy today, like at Christmas, a little ping-pong ball like they left in other**

**shops, the fire's coming from downstairs, that's for certain, what's
that got to do with anything, the store's on fire and I can't get out.**
*That building's a fire-trap; SHE knows that, she wouldn't be so stupid
as to stay upstairs.* **We should have been more careful, the little bomb
on Galiano was a warning of something big, but who on earth could
have done this?** *it's like an oven in here, I'm soaked in sweat, my
uniform's sticking me, I can't breathe, calm down, Lula, calm down,
it's worse if you panic.* **HIM? Could it be HIM? He was so strange
today; he looked like a robot and was sweating like a pig, like there
was no air-conditioning.** *It must be a fireball by now, what could be
happening?; there's no point having second thoughts now, it's already
done, hang in there now, there's no going back; it's always the same
with me, I do something and then I wish I hadn't; like when you mas-
turbate in a public toilet because the smell of piss and dampness
excites you; that's different, I can't help that; of course you can't, you
could only get it up last time by thinking of that smell, and then you
wanted to kill the girl, as if it was her fault; but this is different, I did
what I had to do, I'm not blind, I know what's happening here...it's
getting hotter all the time, it' will be an inferno in here soon, my
eyes won't stop watering, if I could just get back up to the 5th floor,
maybe there isn't so much smoke up there, how do I get up there
though if the stairs are blocked? Easy, Lula, easy, maybe the firemen
are already out there, Ada must know El Encanto is on fire, I wonder
what time it is, I was supposed to meet her at 11 o'clock, at least
Luisa got the clothes for the nursery schools out, those bastards
couldn't burn everything, it must have been HIM, he looked like he
hadn't slept, he was shining with sweat and was pale like he was
sick. Isora and Luisa must have gotten out. Will they know I'm still
in here?** *the floor's scorching, I can feel it through my boots, my feet
are burning, there's no oxygen in here, they say when it's very hot
even the air catches fire, what's could be happening out there?* **I bet
Ada's down there, with Ravelo and Robin, I told Ada that I would
go and get something to eat after I'd checked the 5th floor, Ravelo
will be exhausted after those 72 kilometers, the flames are reaching
the shelves, well, there's nothing else to do then, I can hardly breathe,
I don't know how people can set fire to themselves, what time could**

24

it be? My eyes are killing me, when I asked HIM for the Los Cinco Latinos *record he almost dropped it. Ada will look after Robin and mother, when the shelves catch fire that will be the end, of course it must have been HIM, when Pepe asked him for a cigarette he said he didn't have one and went white as a sheet, it must have been HIM, what time is it? I can't see the clock, I never asked Elena why she grabbed the wall clock when they took that photo, what made her do it? that's why I came out with that daft smile, HE was watching the clock all afternoon, why didn't you realize sooner Lula? he waited until closing time to place the bomb, I'm so thirsty, my God, so thirsty, my throat's dry, I'm going mad with thirst, I wish I could be on the Malecon letting the waves soak me to the skin, we used to go to there when the kids were small, they used to love chasing the crabs on the wall, I wonder where that photo is? Erik will hear of my death before he gets the letter I sent him the other day, funny; everything I told him will be over and gone when he reads that letter, even I'll be dead, there must be some way out, calm down, Lula, you know there isn't; HE must be down there in the crowd, watching the store burn, knowing I'm in here, burning, maybe he's on the run, but they'll catch him, God I hope they catch him...

*Now we're heading for the coast, I can feel the sea air, just a while now and they'll be there waiting for me, as soon as I give the signal they'll come and pick me up, for sure, no one passes that way at this time of night, as soon as I see the boat I'll jump in the sea, once I'm in the water I'm safe, why the hell did he stop here? come on, out now, just a bit to walk, hurry up and don't ask questions...***Maria del Carmen was right, she never liked him, calm down Lula, calm down and think, time's running out any minute now the roof will collapse, you can't carry on much longer, you're as hot as the walls and there's nowhere left to go, everything's burning, Lula, everything's burning, and there's nothing you can do, when the flames finish with the shelves they'll come for you, you can't stop them Lula, you should have realized in time that HE was the enemy, he said those anonymous calls were nothing, he laughed in your face when you talked about the library and then gave you money on the sly for the Mayarí school.** *I was always straight with you, I gave you everithing you asked* *for, don't forget that now, did I do the signal right? ...I can't see a boat...***It was so obvious Lula, but you got distracted and didn't notice, HE knew everything was pointless because he knew the store would burn and you in it, Lula, he must be laughing now, thinking about you getting toasted***...no, that's not it, the store had to burn, but you're there because you wanted to be, don't blame me...***not laughing, no, he must be shitting in his pants, he knows that if they catch him he'll go to the firing squad they will catch him...****I can't see the boat, fucking bastard, I can't believe they've double crossed me, I'll kill Mario if they don't come!* **Erik, come here, Daddy's going to take our picture with Robin, go back a bit to get us all in, don't worry Ada, I'll come down and we'll get something to eat when I've finished checking, pick me up at 11, where are the batteries? This flashlight doesn't work...***what the hell's the matter with this flashlight? I can't see any boat. They've left me, shit, they left me!...***Isora, can you get me some new batteries? Go on Maria Luisa, take the clothes for the kids, they are waiting for them, remember the meeting is at three tomorrow, see you soon Juan!, I'll see you in a couple of days, Ravelo, put two pairs of socks on, so those boots don't rub. Mama, I'll be late for lunch, tell Robin to study, he's got a test tomorrow, if Ada comes tell her to wait for me, at 11, Ada, I'll see you at 11...*

On April 13th 1961, the largest department store in Cuba was destroyed with two packets of incendiary explosives brought in from the United States by terrorists of Cuban origin working for the CIA.

LEGEND First came the blue bird, the dream ended and life began.

It hasn't stopped raining all morning. An intermittent rain, a thin rain drizzling over the Ceiba and running elegantly over the soil. Ceibas in the rain look like women from another place, old wives coming back to the hill with their purchases from the plains. Next to the Ceiba there is a tree that I don't know the name of, a strange tree, large and at the same time slender; tall with branches from a dark jungle. It's not from here. It's from somewhere between Pernambuco and Tierra del Fuego. A tree from cold or warm forests, brought here by the winds of fate. Tree of illusion, space for light and innocent rain.

The house is a thousand meters away, intangible. The place where I recited poems as a child, where I taught the cabbalistic alphabet, the subtle tangle of signs. A hut like the ruins of a palace made of cinnabar palm wood. A Chinaman's shack. A house that talks to me of the lives of Pedro, his wife, the children, the previous tenants who refuse to become ghosts until night falls.

- I want to see you, but I can only hear you. You talk and you whisper as if you were at church, or the cinema -the house tells me.

It's true; the world is like a film, filled with carnivorous flowers devouring the images in your memory. That's why you have to be quick with your

29

memories. The river is a bit down from the house, the silvery stream, spring waters. The next door neighbor's daughters watch me swim. Maria is going to be my girlfriend. She has green eyes that change with the passing clouds. Maria Bonita with braids and the lips of a romantic gypsy. I haven't told her yet that I love her. In eternity, you have to be patient in showing your feelings. Her sisters beg me to talk to her.

- Call her "love"! - says the little one.
- Call her "flower" and she'll kiss you!-says the other.

The three girls walk away laughing and leave me in the river. I swim towards the end of the current, where the big rock is. Pedro says this is where the invisible doctors live. I tell him again and again that none of that is real, a hoax and superstition; but he insists that they live there, and that they intone their chants and show the routes to mountain herbs that cure the flesh of men.

I listen carefully to the rock. I can hear cymbals and tabors, Chinese bugles. I can hear a voice, the magic of liquid images; a fertile voice foretelling the arrival of the night and the dangers of the river path, the only true path to both death and gratitude.

- I cannot believe what you say, I am the teacher- I tell him.
- Teaching poetry is believing in me- answers the invisible voice.

The afternoon goes by undisturbed; a bronze, an afternoon of oak heart; a slight air of anxiety, like under the salt docks; a delicate reverberation over the tree tops. That humming wind attracts all noises: gunfire of men in their battles, trembling trains on the tracks. It brings the smell of vegetation and life forged with infinite questions. Where am I heading, exquisite afternoon? Where am I taking the memories of me and mine in Havana? Can that train take me to Pernambuco, to the roots of the tree, by the Ceiba? Will this listless rain ever stop and leave us an open sky with a bright and inclement desert sun? What joy to live short, intense lives, simply being mortals and watching the day's profiles repeatedly march alongside us under the lights of compassion!

I return home. The dying light reincarnates the night. The twilight's promise is fulfilled. A pig waits on the threshold of the hut, foreseeing the same old litany. Pedro, his wife, his children have all become ghosts. My kerosene lamp is lit in the front room. I can smell fried bananas, salted meat, native cooked rice spiced with coriander.

- The shooting's over. They are running now - says Pedro.

- What if they come here? - asks his wife.
- I'll confuse them with talk.
- You've never been good with words.
- Today I have to be good - replies Pedro.

We eat; I get the lion's share and am embarrassed. Pedro's children don't say a word; silent images, they don't speak or eat, only stare at me as if I were dead.

- They used to talk in the other life - says the woman.
- They can't now, they're scared - Pedro says.
- When the coffee ripens we'll leave this hill- says the woman.
- We'll go to Havana with the teacher- says Pedro lying to himself.
- How long can fear last? - I ask staring back at the children.
- A lifetime. There are fears that last a whole lifetime - Pedro replies.
- Where does fear come from? - asks the woman.
- Anywhere. But now it is out there, crouching in the hills - he says.
- They might not come today - I comfort myself.
- Don't deceive yourself. They will come. Every night's the same. I will talk to them today. Maybe today I can convince them.

Class began after dinner. Pedro and his wife are fluent readers after so much repetition. He never removes his old wide-brimmed hat. She looks at him like she was looking at a mirror. I barely use the booklet, I prefer poetry. It has taught me a lot. Marti introduced me to Emerson, Whitman and old wretched Casal. I have seen Casal, wandering around. His bones were dragged away by the dogs of rain; his grave is empty. That's why you can see him roaming about. But our story is different, and it has nothing to do with Casal.

- Just a few seconds left - says the first kid, his only words.
- There's the noise - says the other, his only words.

The same bellowing, night after night, the pig's death rattle as they kill it in front of the hut. Then they come in, break my books, smash my lamp, force the kids into the same corner, Pedro's wife begs compassion. Always the same. Pedro tries to talk and they shut him up. They ask me if I am the teacher. I don't say yes or no. The chief sings the chorus of some poem. His voice is sweet. Isn't fate strange? This man has a sweet voice when he sings.

They pull us all out into the night, the moon is charmed, there are three moons in the sky, round and gleaming and staring at us. The pig has already

31

been gutted and they take it with us. Pedro goes ahead, stumbling, crawling, trotting. I am the prey; no-one touches me, the singing chief's beloved prey.

We are right by the Pernambuco tree now, he is about to say something and no longer feels the breeze. They are beating Pedro already. I can hear the crackle of his skin, like smacks over a kettledrum. The chief has stopped singing. Now he talks of guilt.

- Who has ever seen letters where there are only mountains? - he says and vents his anger on me. I no longer feel pain after so many years of beatings. Perhaps that makes them madder. They try everything, except pity, from sharp blows to dragging me with a rope tied to my neck. They don't care of my flesh, they don't care about it. I am not their meal, so they don't care about my flesh.

- See what they've done to me! - I feel Pedro's complaints as if he was shaking his hat to the wind. Nobody listens to him, just me. He swings in one of the branches of the Pernambuco tree.

- Now finish it! - says the chief, because killing me every night is tiresome for them, and they drag me over the dead leaves. I smell pigs blood on my killers' hands. I am no longer there, but I can still smell the blood. I can see my body rising over the Pernambuco tree. I am next to Pedro, who has finally lost his hat.

The blue bird flies through the first moon, dives into the second and dissolves in the third. Soon I will find Maria Bonita by the river. Something is about to change. There is music in Pedro's hut. Who could visit that house and bring the music of innocent ballerinas? It rains. I see everything from behind this glass, magnetized by the naivety of the wind around these hills. Perhaps tonight they won't kill me and I will live eternally under the spell of innocent dancers and their music.

On the November 26th 1961, gangs working for the CIA brutally tortured and murdered 16 year old Manuel Ascunce Domenech from Havana. Manuel was in the Escambray mountains teaching the locals how to read and write. The corpse of Pedro Lantigua Ortega, a farmer and Manuel's pupil was found next to his.

Mary had a little lamb
Its fleece was white as snow
And everywhere that Mary went
The lamb was sure to go

GO ON BEING ME Neither Pedro nor I had flown before, so we were a bit nervous. We hadn't ever left Cuba before, so we were excited. We'd never been apart from mum and dad and we were truly miserable. We were alone on our First Big Adventure and we had to be brave. *You're going out into the world on your First Big Adventure and you must be brave, just like she I was when I came to Havana to study, and I became a man.* Mum on the other and, couldn't stop crying and squeezing my little sister, who kept saying p*lay, play, play* just like she always does. Mum was wearing dark glasses that I'm sure she'd never worn before, not even on the beach. Other mothers were wearing them too, inside, where there was no sun at all, and they were crying as well. Even a great big man was as crying in front of everyone. *Bi boys don't cry son. Don't worry, we'll all be together again very soon, I promise. This can't last long.* Dad hugged me like I was a very important person, kissed me on the forehead and ruffled my hair. Mum got a bit upset. *Don't mess the boy's hair up, Hernán!* She pulled a comb from her purse and made me a parting here and a parting there and all the time she was looking at me through those great big dark glasses that made her look very funny. She didn't look like my everyday mum. She sighed and stroked my face and I told her *don't cry*

35

mummy, we'll all be together soon. Seeing her cry made me want to cry as well, although I knew we would be back together soon. *Go now,* my dad said, and I was suddenly afraid.

I felt better when I was in the waiting room with Pedro. My mum and dad and little sister were on the other side of the glass, that's true, but they were in a big crowd of people screaming and crying and I didn't like that. I couldn't hear them in the waiting room. I could see them though. People were waving and making signs and pushing each other against the glass. I don't know how it didn't break. They looked like monkeys or clowns and I felt sorry for them, for all the other kids in the waiting room, for Pedro, and I even felt sorry for myself, although I'd been taught that that was bad. *Compassion and mercy are good, pity is bad.* I thought of a game but I never played it. I would make up conversations between the children; the little fish, and their families; the monkeys, by watching all those crazy signs they were making. That'd be great fun, laughing at everybody, I wanted to have fun, but the game seemed wrong, I don't know why. Not to get bored, Pedro and me thought over everything my parents had told me before we left.

Then we climbed into the spaceship to go to the Moon and visit the naughty Martians. Pedro and me were going to kill them and there was going to be a huge war. The Martians were smelly and ugly. They wanted to steal the Moon and take it to Mars and eat it, because that's what Martians eat. From then on it was our duty to be very smart. Up there, there were thousands of dangers waiting for us and bad enemies that wanted to kill us…we were the heroes and the good guys never lose. We had Angelica's Great Power to protect us, and that would make us indestructible and *brave*…like dad said.

I remember now, I'm not in a spaceship. *You're going to another country, my child, and this old black woman is going to pray for you.* Angelica didn't go to the airport. She didn't even come to the door to wave good-bye. Just before we left she got out some coloured necklaces and rubbed me all over with them, like she wanted to scrub me clean. She was talking funny and I couldn't understand her. Then she gave me a kiss and squeezed me really tight. She was whispering *old black women don't cry, old black women don't cry.* Then she said *little man, you're not going without protection. Take Pedro with you. I've put a good spell on him* and I felt happy because Pedro was my friend and my favourite toy. So me and him started to get ready to win the war.

Pedro, the first thing is that we can't take our safety belt off until we land on the Moon. We've got to be careful, the Martians have spies everywhere. If our spaceship blows up... well...dad said it was all very safe and that I must behave so that they can all come quickly. He told me I'm a man already, a very brave man despite my age, and that he was very proud because I would be the key to open the door for the rest of the family. You see Pedro, I'm a man now, I'm the captain and you've got to obey me.

The first order was to get out of the spaceship with me. What spaceship? The airplane. I read in my head *Mi-a-mi, Miami, Inter-na-tio, International, Air-port. Miami International Airport. You see Pedro, we made it to Mayami without getting killed.* The United States didn't look like the Moon and we didn't see any disgusting monsters. Everything seemed very knew and pretty. There was a priest waiting for us. *Hernán Fraga Errasti?* he asked. I nodded but I didn't say anything, *let's go.* Order number two was to follow me. The priest took us to a little bus with 15 or 20 kids and two nuns sat inside. Another girl and a little boy got on after us and the bus drove away. The last two kids were holding hands. The girl was already quite big and the little boy a lot younger than me. He was whining and calling for his mum and the girl sat him on her lap and hugged him. She was kissing his hair. *They are brother and sister, Pedro.* I wanted to sit on someone's lap too. I wanted someone to kiss my hair. She looked like a nice girl. Anyway, I'had to be brave. *You'll be alright over there with the people from the church, they're our people. They '11 look after you,* mum had told me, lovingly as always. I thought the priest was going to ask me how my mum and dad and little sister were, and that he'd give me a fizzy pop, but maybe he forgot with all the rush. The little boy was asleep on his sister's lap and she was watching the road through the window. He was the only one asleep because we were all watching the road and we were all silent. Order number three was to cuddle each other. I watched the scenery very carefully. The trees, the houses, the shops. *Hernán, in a couple of weeks' at the latest we'll all be together again.* So I'd be doing the same journey very soon, but the other way around to pick up my family. I always liked to keep my eyes wide open on journeys, look at everything from all the angles because I was going to be an architect when I grew up, just like dad. *This country is not bad for us, Pedro, there's lots of open space to build skyscrapers and palaces. As soon as the everyone gets here we'll tell them our plan and maybe they'll buy us some land so we can build a castle for when we get older. A castle for me, because I'm a man, and the boss, and one for you as well, because you are my most loyal servant. OK? Order number four is to help me convince them.*

As well as my secret talk with Pedro, I had more time to think over everything my parents had told me. *Be polite, courteous and responsible...study lots... go to church... eat up all your food... write to us... tell us everything in your letters.* That road was never ending. It seemed that this drive was taking longer than the flight and I thought we were maybe going back to Havana. We went through a lot of towns: Kendall, Princeton, and others I don't remember now, but one stuck in my mind: Orange. I started to feel hungry and I couldn't stop looking and thinking. I didn't feel like playing. Eventually we got to Florida City. The little bus turned right and then left, left and then right and stopped in front of some buildings surrounded by a very high fence. *It looks like we're here. Follow me Pedro, we don't need to be afraid of the Martians anymore. We'll be safe here with the church people, you'll see. Trust your Captain, Pedro. Order number five: trust your Captain.*

The big girl's little brother was still half asleep and she had to drag him along. Me and Pedro kept quiet and vigilant, just in case. That place didn't really look as nice as I had imagined. It was very far away from everything else and didn't look anything like my school in Havana. One of the nuns spoke to us and I was very surprised because I thought they were mute. *Mai neim is sor Belen, from de reliyos order Hermanas de San Felipe Neri. Dis is de Florida Citi camppment an...* All us children looked at each other. Neither me nor Pedro could understand a word, I don't think anyone understood. We looked at the other nun, who was younger, but she wasn't even looking at us. Then the big girl asked the nun if she could repeat what she'd said in Spanish and the nun slapped her. *Listen tu mi! Yu mos spik inglisch, ol of yu, inglish language onli. Du yu onderstendit?* We only understood that the nun was very angry, although I didn't really know why. The big girl held her cheek with one hand and her little brother with the other. He started to cry. I held on tight to Pedro, so they wouldn't hurt him, and I stood in front of the nun. *Please, if it isn't too much trouble, we would be very grateful if you could speak in Spanish.* I tried to be very polite but she still smacked me on the ear. *Stiupid chail!* It hurt a lot, in my chest and in my head as well. It was the first time anyone had hit me and I wanted to cry. *Big boys don't cry, Hernán.* My ears were burning and I thought that I preferred the nuns when they were mute. Maybe the children were the mutes now, you couldn't even hear them breathe. I went back to my place with my head ringing.

They are the Martians, Pedro. We're on the Moon and I think the war is going to start any minute. I warned you, they are very dangerous, they've got spies everywhere and now we know they can disguise themselves. We have to be careful my friend. Just stick with me and don't be afraid. The Captain will look after you. It was time to give Pedro Order number six, but I didn't know what to order him. We picked up our bags and followed the rest of the children, girls to one side, boys to another. The big girl's little brother was screaming his lungs out *Mummy! Mummy! I want my mummy! Paula, I want my mummy!* His eyes were all swollen from crying so much and his face was red and soaked in tears. Paula was desperate, she left the girl's line and picked the boy up. *Don't worry, my love, they won't separate us.* Luckily the Martians were at the front and they didn't see her, but when Paula tried to get into our apartment a lady stopped her. They talked in loud voices for a while and then everything was alright because Paula and her little brother took the bunk bed next to mine. *I'm Paula, thanks for trying to help me.* Help her? *I'm Hernán, don't mention it.* I wanted to tell her about the Martians, about my family, about Pedro, but I was afraid to speak Spanish. Then they sent us for dinner in turns. I wasn't hungry and anyway, I didn't like the food they served, so I didn't touch a thing. Sister Belen made me eat in a foreign language a foreign food that wasn't Angelica's. I swear I didn't want to but she forced the egg into my mouth. I felt very bad and then I was sick. I was so ashamed because everyone in the dining room was watching me. *Eat up all your food.* I couldn't, I swear. Sister Belen made me eat again. This time she made me eat the vomit. I thought I was going to faint. I knew that sick was dirty, that only a pig would eat it, but it was already in my mouth and all over my face and hands and I spat it onto Sister Belen. I ran out and went to bathroom to wash my face, to look for Pedro, to write a letter, anything. I ran away.

There was a queue outside our bathroom but everyone moved aside because I stank.

Nobody would ever love me again because I stank, because I had offended Sister Belen, because I didn't eat up all my food. *Nobody in the world will love me anymore* I told the water, that was cold, but felt very good. I lay down next to Pedro and told him what had happened. *We must do something, Pedro, we can't let them win.* I lay there quite calm for the rest of the day until it got dark. I spoke to God too, I asked him to bring my parents very quickly, and little Laura, and even Angelica, or if not, that he send me back to Cuba, or if not…I didn't want to go on being me. Two children interrupted my thoughts *we want you to join our boy scout troop.* I told them to go away. *We're not going, we want you to fight against…they* were pretty mad and I thought I was going to get in trouble again, but Paula arrived with Femandito and she sent the kids to bed. *See you tomorrow, big mouth.* Big mouth?

- Big mouth?
- Yes, they call both of us «big mouths» now. I think its because of what we did on the first day.
- Maybe, but there are some things... I don't know. So many things have happened to me today. I think they might kill me for what I did. When they find out at home...
- Nothing's going to happen to you, and they won't find out at home. But you've got to be careful- she told me as she put Femandito to bed.
- I will behave from now on, Paula – she made me feel safe, like a mother that never tells you off, or a big sister – Hey, this bear is my best friend and he's called Pedro… He has a Great Power.
- What kind of Great Power?
- Do you really want me to tell you?
- Of course.
- Well, he has the Great Power of Angelica, to fight the Martians with.
- Fight the what?
- The Martians. Don't laugh.
- Who are the Martians, Hernán?
- They all are, Paula. The nuns, the priests all of them. They're everywhere and they can disguise themselves. They're very dangerous.

-   They're dangerous alright, but they're not Martians. They're flesh and blood just like you and me.
-   You reckon?
-   I'm sure.
-   Why are they so bad to us?
-   Because we're a nuisance for them.
-   No, Paula, that can't be right. My parents told me they were going to be very nice to
    us and that I should be polite with them. *The people from the church are our people.*
-   And what do you think now, Hernán?
-   I don't know, I guess there has been some kind of mistake and it will all be cleared up tomorrow at school.
-   What school, Hernán?
-   Well...the school where I'm going to study. That's why I'm here, to study lots and lots.
-   No, Hernán, now it's you that are wrong. When you got to the airport, did they ask for your passport?
-   Yes.
-   Did they write anything in it?
-   They put a stamp in it.
-   Did you read what the stamp said?
-   No.
-   Take a look now.

We were whispering to each other because the lights had already been turned off, and we didn't want them to hear us speaking in Spanish. I found my passport and took it to the window to read in the light. I looked outside and saw the Moon. *There's one thing for sure, the Moon is up there and I am down here.* I turned the pages slowly, then stopped and went back to my bunk.

-   The stamp says «refugiado».
-   Do you know what that means?
-   No.
-   Refugee, Hernán, you're a refugee.
-   A what?! I'm a student.

-   Not now, kid. In Cuba you were a student. Here, you're a refugee.
We fell silent because someone started to cry, a girl. You could hear her very well, she was calling to her parents. After a while I spoke in an even lower whisper.

-   Why does everyone cry, Paula?
-   Because they are refugees too and they miss home.
-   What does "refugee" mean?
-   That you've run away from your country and that this country is going to protect you.
-   But I didn't run away from Cuba. My parents sent me here to a private school so that the revolutionaries couldn't wash my brain. They're atheists and communists...
-   Yeah, yeah, and they were going to send us all to Russia to be educated, or eaten...I've heard all that already. But what I've seen here has made me think. My parents didn't think it was going to be like this, no one in my family did, not even me. Now I wonder what Russia would have been like. I don't know if Communism is as terrible as they say, that 'the revolutionaries are barbarians, that they don't even believe in their own mothers. They must follow some saint and I bet they've all prayed some times...they came down from the mountains full of amulets.
-   If you're so smart, Paula, do you think this country will protect us?
-   I don't know, I really don't. I think the most important thing is to survive, to do anything to survive... and stay with Femandito.
-   I know what you mean. I've got to look after Pedro... imagine if my little sister Laura was here...no, it's best not to imagine it...you'll see though, everything will be sorted out tomorrow.
-   How old are you, Hernán?
-   Ten.
-   Well, you're very clever, and very brave. Keep your eyes open and you'll see for yourself. Now, go to sleep..
-   Do you really think I'm *brave?*
-   Yes, very brave.
-   Sleep tight, Paula.
-   You too, Hernán.

I lay quiet. Femandito and Pedro were already asleep. It had been a busy day and they were only little. The cries of other children didn't wake them but they made me feel very sad. I tossed and turned in that narrow, hard bed. The voices in my head wouldn't stop. *Old black women don't cry, old black women don't cry.*

- Paula, can you hear them?
- Yes.
- Will they ever be quiet?
- I don't know
- Will you bless me?
- God bless you, Hernán.
- God bless you, Paula.

She definitely was a very nice girl, just a bit confused about some things. Russia was hell, the revolutionaries devils, Communism was bad and so it was better for everyone if I went to study in the United States. The whole family would be better in the United States, today had just been a little mistake. Me, a refugee? Refugee? No. Paula didn't know what she was talking about. OK, so I exaggerated about the Martians, *boys' things* like Angelica used to say to defend me. But me, a refugee!? OK, so I couldn't explain that stamp in my passport, but who was lying to me then? The Church? My family? My parents? Why? Didn't they love me anymore? And if they did love me, why did they tell me...my head was like a box of lead soldiers all shouting "why!", "what for!" "but". My head was heavy, all those soldiers crashing into each other up there. My eyes were heavy too, they burned...

I don't know how I got to sleep, but I remember waking up with a start. *Pedro! Pedro! Where are we?* I realised in a flash and jumped out of bed. *Quick, Pedro, it's late already.* Paula and Femandito were already gone. I bumped into them in the dining room. I was very hungry and I'd woken up ready to be polite and helpful. *Today is the big day my friend, let's study!* I felt very good and I knew that things would start to fit into place at last. But the mess in the camp confused me a bit. Nobody could tell us anything, most of the kids didn't have any books with them, I couldn't see any teachers. I began to suspect something was wrong. I followed some girls that were carrying their schoolbooks. I followed them into a big classroom full of different coloured desks, with kids of all ages, from all years and only one teacher. I had a very bad feeling about it. There was such a racket and mess, but I couldn't stand the idea that Paula was right. I couldn't stand it.

My ears started to bum again and I wanted to scream my lungs out. But I stayed still and silent. I didn't want to be smacked again and I never wanted to breathe again. Something was going to burst inside me, I felt it very strong, like a dizziness I'd never felt before. I ran. I ran just like the day before, looking for something, anything familiar. There was nothing. I ran far away. I ran and I fell and I ran and fell again. I hurt myself and they hurt me.

Irreversible damage, Pedro. The Orders began to fade away, and then one day they
stopped altogether. I didn't need them anymore. I didn't need even you, or the great power.

Only I mattered, me and all my pain. The different images blend into one and I can no longer separate them. That's the way I remember my first day in this country "willing to protect me". Or maybe these scenes happened gradually over the next 11 years. Pedro, don't trust a memory that denies even itself Two weeks that lasted 11 years or one first day that stretches from one decade to the next. Closed internal doors, blurred but inerasable memories from my first childhood, and all that stunted love that I can't cast off nor remember clearly. No one can turn back time to feel yesterday's heartbeat with the same intensity. Nothing obliges us to remember the "us" of before. Now, lean over my son's cradle, just like you leant over mine to watch me sleep. Now see the failed tailor I have been ever since with his emotions snipped and backstitched and crisscrossed with loose threads. I omitted certain details, Pedro, I fixed them on my sewing machine so you wouldn't worry. Just like I did in my letters to my parents "couldn't be better, mum", "thanks dad", "come whenever you can, lam very happy" "I've bought Laura hundreds of dolls", "give Angelica a kiss from me"...I didn't want them to worry but I think I failed. I never told you the full story of our reunion, Pedro. My journey back to the airport, like you know, wasn't as I had imagined. I'd left the castles and palaces and architecture and cement far behind, but I was still very excited and full of plans for a peaceful future, just what we all deserved. I can still see my parents and my sister scanning the shadows, nervous, searching for me, stood right before me, the worker... until I called their names. I can still hear, Pedro, my mother's dead phrase of nine years ago "You're not my son! You're not my son!" Maybe she was right. Little Hernán died when he left Cuba, and I have buried him deep. I have managed to scrape together a man from what was left so that, despite everything, I can at least go on being me.

The CIA has implemented psychological warfare to create an atmosphere of confusion in Cuba and undermine support for the Revolution. One of their ploys, known as 'Operation Peter Pan', spread the lie that the Cuban government was going to take away parents' custody of their own children.

To Teresita Fornaris
and Juan Carlos Rodríguez

CHOCOLATE MILKSHAKE

1

The man who was going to be poisoned found a gray hair when he looked in the mirror, his first gray hair and spent almost five minutes stroking it and wondering whether to pluck it out or leave it in his tangled beard. He knew the popular myth that if you pluck a gray hair more come out and he wasn't very happy with the image of a young man with a political life to sprout a salt and peppered beard. The man who was going to be poisoned played with the gray hair, stroked it, stretched it, hid it in the black hairs of the beard and looked at himself from different angles. The mirror also looked back. First with his own piercing eyes; then he looked full into the mirror, indifferent; later he took in the quicksilver, with the frame, with the small light bulbs that bordered the edge. The mirror and the man who was going to be poisoned knew each other very well; perhaps that is why the mirror knew before him, the fate of his first gray hair. It knew even before the curly black hairs that wrapped around it. When the man who was going to be poisoned donned his cap and took two steps back and smiled sure of the decision he had taken, the mirror already knew that the gray hair was the forerunner of others.

2

The glass that was going to be used to poison the man of the recently discovered gray hair was a common glass, transparent and tall, one of those the waiters called a 14 ounce glass. If there was any distinguishing marks these could be the ridges that broke its perfect cylindrical exterior, fine edges to break up the circular reflection of the liquid or to help grasp it. But, after all, this did not make it exclusive. There were, at least, eleven glasses with these same ridges, they were made of the same glass, occupied the same station, the same shelves, the same tables, the same glass holders, the same counter, the same water faucets, the same hands of the same waiter. Consequently, eleven glasses could be protagonists of the poisoning. This created tension in the cafeteria. The man who was going to be poisoned could enter at any moment, any day, and it would be pure chance which glass would be picked. Or no, there wouldn't even be a selection. Chance would decide which glass would receive the lethal potion, which would be the protagonist of this story. Then, this glass could only do what others do who are implicated in the poisoning: wait. If there was something that gave him confidence was thinking that the last two times the man who was going to be poisoned entered the cafeteria, it had been it and no other, the glass Santo had used to serve his favorite drink. Only it would know, and no other, before anyone how the man was going to be poisoned while he savored the perfect mixture of cocoa and milk, how he savored it with excited breath and looking strait ahead, over the top edge of the froth. It had been the one to discover the first gray hair in the beard of the man who was going to be poisoned, and no other. It had been it and no other. So this time, the next time, the final time, it had to be it.

3

The place the chocolate milk shake lover, who was going to be poisoned, was the cafeteria of a Havana hotel, but not one of the little hotels of the many that lit the mythical nights of Havana during the fifties, nor the old stately colonial hotels, but a modern hotel, an impressive skyscraper inaugurated by Batista towards the end of nineteen fifty eight, the last purchase of the Hilton chain, this time in the very heart of Havana, that, it should not be forgotten, was the heart of everything. The hotel where the man with the

48

recently discovered gray hair was going to be poisoned, had changed the traditional view of Havana, with its mere presence of concrete and great windows. It height and grandeur had for ever shadowed those around: the trees looked small and the walls of what had once been the Reina Mercedes hospital that became the Cabaret Nocturnal and then the famed Coppelia; the small apartment buildings; the small Radiocentro; minute buses that went up and down 23rd street along L street; the taxis look ridiculous and the people walking along La Rampa, like ants; thousands of two legged ants listening to a portable radio, of any size, the men to follow the National Ballgame Series, the women to listen to the last hit of Tito Gómez with the Riverside or Meme Solís, others with nothing more important to do than look up at the building and count its floors, drinking Hatuey or Coca–Cola or, why not, savoring a chocolate milk shake prepared by Santos, perhaps the same glass used by the man who was going to be poisoned, the perfect mixture of Brazilian cocoa and bottled milk.

4

The milk that was to be used in the poisoned milk shake had arrived at the cafeteria of the hotel that very morning in a refrigerated bulk liquid container and had been stored in a refrigerated tank. It's surprising to see how customs change and how the relations of man with his basic products are conditioned. In Havana, during the first decade of the XX century, for example, cows still wandered with their bells clanging and mooing in the morning along the main streets of the city, leaving their droppings in the kerosene smelling puddles and old rain, their hoof prints left in the mud and tar, in the midst of the rails of the streetcars and heels of the pedestrians. But more than the fly festered cow dung the people from Havana knew that the early mooing and clanging bell announced the arrival of the milk. Then, with the thirsty punctuality of the family man, everyone opened their doors and windows, gates and railings to place their canteens under the cow udder enjoying that sound of the white liquid on metal, the beautiful froth overflowing. But of course during the next decade Havana changed very much and very fast, the city spread out everywhere (especially up) uncontrollably. By the early fifties very few streetcars crossed the city, the tar in the streets had hardened and paving appeared in the great avenues. By then the cows no longer mooed at the doors of the homes, nor did the carts carrying sugar cane cross the heart of the great city offering sugar cane juice in every corner; by that time the National Capital, the Civic Plaza and the Havana Hilton had been completed; this was another Havana, a city populated by gangsters and pimps, whores and soldiers, tourists from the US and Black boxers, of day laborers with their sharpened *guámparas* and dented canteen, and gambling and sugar magnates, remnants of the colonial sugarocracy that is now Yankee, with Vedado mansions and children studying in the high schools, naïve contenders to enroll in the Ruston Academy; yes, Havana was another, a city marked by electoral wars and political chicanery, a city where the cows became symbols of prosperity or misfortune. Cartoons of skinny famished cows appeared among sensational headlines, cows who gave no milk cows that had dried up, they seemed taken straight from Mauthausen. The inhabitants of Havana had to adapt to the silence of six in the morning in their narrow streets. No mooing, no clanging of bells, and certainly no cow dung in the paths, or broken up sidewalks; certainly not the stream of milk hitting the bottom of the family canteen. Now milk came bottled. This was progress. No one saw the full cow udder being emptied. Now the children open their eyes and already the milkman had full bottles of milk on the counters. The cows no longer existed. Milk was a separate and independent product. It didn't matter if it was for a newborn baby, for an ill person's diet, for clients of a luxury hotel. Milk arrived at the hotels in large refrigerated canteens. From there it was served at breakfast, with coffee, or with cocoa; or alone as a refreshing drink; or in milk shakes, with different flavors, of tropical fruits, of strawberry, of vanilla, of ice cream, of chocolate …, this latter was, undoubtedly the star flavor, preferred by children and adults, men and women, tourists and natives, poor and rich, white and Blacks, politicians and pedestrians; the milk and chocolate was set free from the cow and the cocoa plantations; milk and chocolate were mixed restfully, fusing to perfection, a cross of texture and flavor and aroma, an incomparable treat. Santos knew it. And the man who was going to be poisoned also knew it. The Central Intelligence Agency knew it. And Polita Grua. And Mongo Grau. And Manolo Campanioni. And each and every twelve fourteen ounce and imperceptibly ribbed glasses. Only the ice cubes didn't know because the ice became part of the fateful milk shake that night in March of sixty three, and it was still not ice, but water, only water (and water does not think as we all know).

5

Chocolate that was going to be used to kill the man with the recently discovered gray hair was one of the few products that continued to arrive by sea to the Havana port. Behind was the time of great fleets from northern ports, when thousands of Havana inhabitants rested on the seawall, Malecon, to watch them dock and children ran after the sailors – innocent reminder of a Havana besieged by corsairs and Dutch and English pirates – polychrome Greek, Spanish or US sailors who, once disembarking, went to the whore barrio, to change the bitter flavor of herring and *aguardiente* for the cheap carmine colored liquor and lascivious perspiration, leaving on the skin of the Cuban girls their remains of anger and lust, all the months of onanism. They were robust men, brothel flesh, men who knew nothing of politics or revolutions. They never understood because, all of a sudden, they were forbidden to walk the streets of Havana, of betting in its casinos and venting their anger in the brothels. They didn't understand who these *barbudos* were, who frightened the bosses of the large shipping companies and even more; who were the gringos to decide that the Veracruz port yes, the Maracaibo port yes, the Cartagena de Indias yes, as in colonial times, but it was completely forbidden to set sail past the Havana Morro, forbidden, very forbidden, don't even think about it, leaving many of them with their ripe tongues and tense groins, including those sailor who couldn't say good–bye to their latest native acquisition. Nothing, that's it. Forbidden to unload their merchandize in this port, forbidden to disembark. Zero mulattas, zero rumba, zero Habanos, zero everything because Havana is going through a bearded epidemic that is more dangerous than cholera, than European plagues, an epidemic that not only affects persons, but buildings also, companies, industries, radio and television stations, never seen before, the worse epidemic that has struck humanity affecting human beings, but not this one, this one affects walls, papers, windows, rolls of money, stamps, electric cables, means of transportation, everything is contaminated, contracts die out, working days die out, rents are dead, laws are dead, total chaos, a catastrophe and explained, as clear as that, the sailors are calmed down, they accept reluctantly, they like a good time very much, yes, but not to such an extent, they are sailors not martyrs, so Havana is in quarantine so we'd best continue to jerk off, play poker, dominoes, dice among ourselves, on deck or in the bunks,

we'll get to safer ports,
yes, yes, this will pass
if the Americans have gotten involved, with the advances of medicine in the past years no epidemic will last forever; the sailors delight in their memories of previous years,
ah, the summer of fifty six,
ah, the spring of fifty seven
its true that there were rumblings already of this epidemic of the barbudos in Oriente, yes, but it hasn't reached the whorehouses of China Town nor the casinos of the Habana Riviera nor, also those of the Habana Hilton, and if they did get there they blended in very well, there was a firm and claiming argument,
tropical climates are prone to all kinds of epidemics … there is no need to worry.

But of course, five years have passed since that Christmas of fifty eight where the epidemic of the barbudos spread to all the island and three years since the gringos declared complete quarantine, absolute isolation of the infirm island. They have been five long years, five years without drinking Hatuey or Arechabala, not smoking Partagás or H. Upman. It's too much. For an English sailor used to impregnable beaches in other places, it's too much. For a Greek sailor, descendants of Ulysses it's too much. For the great grandchildren of Vasco de Gama, it's too much. Even for a Brazilian sailor although their country has exuberant beaches, luscious women, candles for Ochun, sensual dances, it's also too much. That's why there was almost a mutiny aboard the *O Samba* and although it may not have been in fact, at least in spirit it was, mostly in the holds, a great ruckus of dissatisfied sailors led by someone called Sebastiao de Oliveira, a huge Black, strong, who did not accept that this was the last shipload of chocolate from pier four to be unloaded at Havana because the O Samba, according to the captain would never dock again in any Cuban port until the epidemic is over. Sebastiao de Oliveira was very upset, he was grabbing the pike and screaming that he was going to bed an indescribable woman from Guanabacoa, arguing that chocolate was rich in caffeine, phosphorus, magnesium, iron, potassium, calcium, vitamin E, thiamine, theobromine and tannin, that its consumption would be efficient to get rid of the epidemic. Poor Sebastiao de Oliveira, who also stuttered and in spite of his size, was pitied and laughed at nipping the mutiny in the bud. But, of course, he was right although he never knew it. Without knowing it Sebastiao forecast the use of chocolate in the plot to kill the man who was going to be poisoned. We still don't know how the thoughts of Sebastiao fell on the ears of Polita Grau, on the minds of the Mafiosi John Roselli and the CIA agents William Harvey and Robert Maheu, perhaps it was a simple historic coincidence but what is true is that the CIA, the Mafia and the members of Brothers thought the same as the angry Brazilian sailor: that chocolate could end the epidemic. Among them, through telephone calls and invisible messages in the style of James Bond, they hid the poison inside the properties of caffeine and tannins because of their capacity to mask the other flavors in any mixture. In a chocolate milk shake, for example, it would be difficult to discover, mostly if the milligrams needed were mixed and beaten by the elegant hands of Santos de la Caridad, the efficient Santito, one of the best waiters of the cafeteria of the former Habana Hilton. It was clear, decided: it was perfect. Chocolate was the solution against that epidemic of the *barbudos*.

6

The poison that was going to be used to kill the man with the recently discovered gray hair was not like any other. The CIA did not want anything like criminal literature, nothing ridiculously irrational. When Johnny Roselli and Robert Matheu met in the Brown Derby restaurant in Beverly Hills, they still didn't know what the poison would be like. Neither knew Santito nor his flare for making milk shakes; neither thought that Polita Grau could be the *in situ* boss in that carefully planned operation. Only after the meal in the Brown Derby, Johnny Roselli, with the alias of John Rawiston contacted some people in Miami and presented himself as a Wall Street business man interested in Cuban nickel. This John Rawiston speaking in a clear low voice sounding his c's and z's clearly, said

the job had to be well done and cleanly.

At the beginning the CIA was in favor of an assassination in the Roselli style for the pleasure of seeing the man who was going to be poisoned, be shot down in the midst of his people, before the cameras to later broadcast that he had been shot by his own people, tired of this communist epidemic. Of course, Rawiston–Roselli, specialist hit man, disagreed, that it would be difficult to recruit someone for such a dangerous operation.

Rawiston–Roselli preferred a poison that leaves no traces, as suggested by his direct boss, Salvatore Giancana. Then, gradually the idea of poison took force. In the CIA laboratories, real artists in the work with toxic substances, thought, proposed... Some poisons were rejected because they were not soluble in water; others, like cyanide, because its effect was in minutes and, consequently, the Fourth Type was easily discovered... also (Scheider thought)

it could be like Rasputin where Yusupov put it in a sweet wine and the carbon of the cyanide combined with the wine's sugar neutralizing the effect.

Arsenic wasn't a good choice either because in spite of its aspect (a white and insipid powder, odorless, looking like sugar or flour), no, its symptoms were too well known. They had to continue to think. Then one windy winter afternoon, just right for a warm winter coat, Scheider appeared with the ideal, final proposal, the magic capsules. He got comfortable in the armchair, fixed his collar, spoke of the *botulinum* or botulism toxin, the only toxin that fulfilled all expectations when tested in monkeys. The words spoken by Scheider sounded like heavenly music to everyone, hesitant to interrupt him. Scheider tried to be really clear, with little technicalities,

explained that the botulin is a botulism toxin, the disease caused by canned meats.

He spoke without gestures, barely moving his lips,

adding that it was used in spastic paralysis in small space timed doses,

while the others looked at him like schoolboys and Scheider made only one movement: his pupils moving from one to another, while he explained

its usefulness in medicine, but lethal, devastating with only 0,02 milligrams.

His listeners knew nothing of milligrams but the adjectives, "lethal" and "devastating" certainly did. Bingo! Great euphoria of the threesome. Now Santos Trafficante and Tony Varona joined the group forming a happy pentagon, five minds and bodies and glasses of whisky, five men with only one voice and one thought.

It is perfect.... You are the best Mr. Scheider.

Months later, while in Miami Beach they were all together for the Floyd Patterson–Ingemar Johansson fight for the heavyweight crown, while boxing fans shouted with glee or horror, according to their favorite, a short distance from the ring another meeting was underway with the threesome Maheu–Roselli–Giancana. This time in a suite of the Fontainebleau Hotel. It was still a scalene triangle: Salvatore Giancana was the sharp hypotenuse, the powerful boss, the one who made decisions even if these came from the Agency, represented by Robert Maheu. Comfortably seated, oblivious to the counts of protection on Patterson – they were beginning their own count down, the final one, for the man who was going to be poisoned – Johnny Roselli spoke with discretion and professionalism, Robert Maheu repeated his favorite phrase,

now or never

and Salvatore Giancana kept his eyes on the door, in silence. The suite had red rugs, tasseled lamps, huge windows, large mirrors reflecting the triangle from different angles. They were happy, sitting in a triangular order, drinking whisky and weighing all the possibilities. Suddenly the door opened to let in the one they were expecting, Santos Trafficante with a mysterious gray haired man and dark glasses hiding his eyes. Seeing them, the three knew at once, it was finally the one. In other words, the First Guy, the point of the plot that would lead them to the Guy of Truth, the waiter of the Habana Libre Hotel cafeteria. The Maheu–Roselli–Giancana threesome welcomed the First Guy with hand shakes who responded to all returning the welcome saying

I am Tony Varona,

losing his alias and was identified with his name,

I am Tony Varona.

He settled into an Elizabethan armchair, crossing his legs and lighting up an Habano. He had the air and harshness of when he had financial interests in Cuba, during the Prío presidency, becoming one of the rivals of Meyer Lansky in Havana and Florida. All were lounging comfortably but tense, the scalene triangle looking at the First Guy, Santos Trafficante moderately demonstrating his rank in Florida and the First Guy waiting to hear the details of the mysterious Operation Poison. At once, Maheu opened a black briefcase that was on the table and without uttering a word, placed ten thousand dollars on the knees of Tony Varona, it is just an advance

he said, while Tony Varona seemed to smell rather than see wad of bills. It was a conditioned reflex developed in the Havana casinos. While the other gamblers and croupiers handled the money, weighed it or looked at it longingly, he smelled it and calculated the amount of dollars. Cuban pesos didn't smell the same, or Francs, or Pounds Sterling. Now Tony Varona spread his nostrils, half closed his eyes with pleasure and repeated to himself,

the advance is all right.

Then Maheu interrupted his smelling inspection, took his hand, keeping it open, palms up, and placed three small capsules in the center, capsules that looked innocent enough, more like a medicine. This time Tony Varona didn't smell them; instead he looked at them, weighed them in his hand, and touched them. The Maheu–Roselli–Giancana triangle then began to explain simply and calmly, with professionalism, of what the Operation consisted, except the participation of Polita Grau, Manolo Campanioni and Santos de la Caridad, Santito, who would be the Second, Third and Fourth Parts of the puzzle, respectively. They couldn't explain this because they still didn't know it. It would be The First Guy, Tony Varona, who would pick the following ones. It was all clear, detailed, because Tony Varona would have to explain it further up.

Don't worry,
this leaves no clues,
the symptoms appear after
six hours and can take up to six days,

Maheu explained getting comfortable in his chair and taking a sip of Kardhu.

The sooner the
symptoms appear, the surer the death,

Roselli explained without taking his eyes off Maheu, looking for support. Tony Varona asked nothing, just listened.

The man would continue his normal life,
give his speeches, have no fever but,
suddenly his mouth would be dry, he would see double,
would not be able to see up front, have trouble swallowing, and would
not be able to mutter a
word

56

and now they couldn't hold back their snickers imagining the man who was going to be poisoned in silence, trying to deliver a speech with sign language. Santos Trafficante asked two or three questions, keeping his distance as if sensing the doubts of Tony Varona in his altar of Great Capo. Roselli answered all, sometimes in the voice of Roselli and others with the voice and gestures of Rawiston, always with a smirk on his lips, as if the plan were funny or imagining how happy his bosses back in the Agency would be once they heard how all was going. Now, with a common pause, the five lifted their hands and drank, five mouths savoring the refreshing Kardhu. The first to break the silence was Maheu;

they had to get them into Cuba as soon as possible,
but Tony Varona was thinking of something else, curiosity of a capo,
I suppose.

Where did they come from?
It was now Rawiston who jumped to answer, silencing Roselli, expertly,

what does it matter,
but Maheu was more diplomatic, he was an operations expert for the Agency;

they were prepared by Dr. Scheider,
our best chemist,
speaking in a persuasive tone, he knew it wasn't enough just to convince the First Guy explaining that the poison took several days to have its effect, that it had no symptoms and left no clues; he knew that this First Guy had to convince many people and that the main feature of success was in the anonymity and surprise but also to insure that the perpetrator would get out unharmed. He didn't go into details, he didn't explain that the botulin was derived from a bacteria called Ricin extracted from the Castor Bean; he didn't speak of spores, nor of vegetable cell nor of toxins; no he wasn't Scheider nor was Tony Varona, Santito, so he simply explained that botulin was soluble in any liquid and left no clues, it had no taste or strange smell. There was a pause and, suddenly, they all began to laugh and began disorderly comments, as if everything was ready, as if they could see the man who was going to be poisoned drinking his milk shake, suffering muscular contractions, progressive paralyses, going mute, pupils that did not react to the light, drooping eyelids, inert thorax, falling down. The five were talking at the same time. They all had more or less important reasons to kill the man

who was going to be poisoned. Maheu, even, quoted wise words expressed by Kissinger, saying

why do we have
to stand apart watching
how the country became communist
as a result of the irresponsibility of its own people
and all that was missing was a clapping of hands; in a short time they would be part of the History of America; they, the five, would be received in the Oval Office and would dine in Camp David, without ignoring the great business deals that would open up in Havana. Yes, all right, Okay, making victory signs with their fingers. They served another round of Kardhu and toasted for a Free Cuba, a toast that where only the glasses of Polita and Santito were missing; she's now meeting with her comrades of Rescate[1], he's setting up the Osterizer for milk shakes, adding ice, sugar, chocolate.

7

A chocolate milk shake is just simply a refreshing drink, pleasant tasting, harmless; no one could suspect that it would be used for an assassination, not even the man who was going to be poisoned, experienced in these kinds of things, used to distrust and protect himself against the fierce will of the enemy. Not even his Orishas[2], although everyone was sure that he was protected, that he was the legitimate son of Chango[3], the warrior orisha. Not even his personal guard, watchful men with many hands, many legs and many ears. No one. The March night of sixty three when the man who was going to be poisoned arrived in the Havana Libre, thirsty, with his disheveled beard, cap tilted back, and the chocolate milk shake was ready to be mixed with the botulin with no one suspecting anything. It was the time when the man who was going to be poisoned ate anywhere when he was hunger, without any precautions. He even had a suite on the 21st floor in the Habana Libre to catch a few hours sleep. The enemy knew this. Also, the

[1] Rescate= Brothers to the Rescue, a counterrevolutionary organization based in Florida.
[2] Orishas = spirits of African religions
[3] Chango = a warrior orisha represented as St. Barbara in the Catholic religion.

inexperience of his Security service was commented in the halls of Langley and the White House.

It isn't so difficult,
the CIA representative repeated in the hall of Polita Grau's house,
although his movements
are random, this very haphazardness
is in our favor,
Polita insisted, in the cottage terrace of Mongo Grau,
the fish dies by the mouth,
Campanioni said sententiously while leaning on the bar of El Recodo, where he liked to go to drink a Rum Collins with Santito, Bartolomé and Saciero, to talk of «business and politics». In that same bar of El Recodo, a week before the poisoning, Santito and Campanioni were on the point of changing the plans, desperate because the man who was going to be poisoned was not showing up in the hotel; that is when they talked of killing the brother of the man who was going to be poisoned, or Che, or Efigenio Ameijeiras who went to El Recodo frequently. When they told Polita of the change, she mentioned it to Capdevilla and Capdevilla informed Tony Varona by phone and Tony Varona told Roselli and Roselli discussed it with William Harvey and Maheu and the latter approved the change informing Polita in a coded message to the CIA station in Havana and then Polita told Campanioni again and he told Santos again, who was going to do it.

So, when the man who was going to be poisoned entered the cafeteria that night in March of sixty three, the conspirators were prepared to abort the plan, or change it for the assassination of some others. So that some one – especially the man who was going to be poisoned – should stop and think of the dangerousness of the chocolate. Three years had passed since the campaign of Parental Rights, but the echoes of Radio Swan were still not turned off, harangues by Pancho Gutierrez continued trying to convince mothers to send their children to the Unite States to save them from the savage communism. Every night Pancho Gutierrez took the mikes of Radio Swan where he harangued the listeners in the name of God, the Family and Democracy, and you could imagine the thick veins in his neck and the perspired forehead. At eight thirty at night thousands of Cubans were glued to their Zenith, like it was when Chibas struck out; like when detective Chang Li Po discovered crimes in spite of changing his r–s for l–s; like when the soap opera *The Right to be Born* kept every one keyed up, some mothers cried, others doubted others were furious with impotence …

Cuban mother, listen to this! The next government law to be passed is to take children from the age of five to eighteen from their parents and when they are returned they will be monsters of materialism … Cuban mothers, don't let them take your child!

He sounded disturbed with a deep hollowed voice,

Cuban mother; the government will take your child away to indoctrinate him with communism! Putting emphasis on the word «indoctrinate» and «communist» stressing the Russian phobia in the Island. From the early years of the sixties there were rumors that in Russia, the womb of pregnant women were bayoneted and the children taken away to indoctrinate them; that in a Havana bay port there was a Soviet boat ready to take the children to Moscow from where they will returned in tins of meat; about fifty mothers from Bayamo had signed a pact to kill the children before handing them over to Castro; rumors of instructions were spread, rumors by the monster Bryan O. Walsh and Polita Grau Alsina, yes that great Polita who all of a sudden became a mother of the homeland, a matron concerned over the millions of innocents who would be killed for tinned meat to fatten the barbudos, the same Polita that years later would take, hide and distribute Scheider's capsules, Polita Grau giving instructions over the telephone to Pancho Gutierrez to prevent «the Russian tragedy» at all costs, to broadcast…

you, Cuban mother, can have your clothing and food taken away and even be killed but your right to raise your own child cannot be taken away by anyone, remember that the most dangerous beast is the mother who protects her cub!

The night they were going to poison the man with the recently discovered gray hair, three years of these events had passed, its true, but it was still mentioned in broadcasts in all spaces and at all times, in whispers, in loud voices and the name of Polita Grau kept coming back to mind. Polita's house was used to issue the visa *wavers* for thousands of children who left by sea and air to the North; the house of Polita was used to study the orders that arrived from Tony Varona, doubts of Maheu and Roselli were answered,

60

everything. 1963 had been named the "Year of Organization" but, there was great confusion in Havana. The city was the center of calls to the sugar cane harvest with songs by Bob Dylan, revolutionary slogans with the sweet ballads of Clara and Mario, the backfires of the militia in the new Volgas, the explosion of petards in some stores, with the last processions of Holy Week. And the man who was going to be poisoned was always everywhere, in the center of everything, on the side, on top, below, the ever-present, loquacious and elusive man. Something strange was happening in 1963: it was as if everyone was young, or as if there were more young persons than ever in Havana than anywhere else. Wherever you looked there were adolescents or post–adolescents going about anxious to do something; the boys showing off their smooth looking getup – *guapitas* – with tight belts and wide trouser cuffs; the women with bows at the neckline with long necklaces, crossed breasted jackets and skirts that went below the knees; all young, younger than ever, with short hair and sailor blouses with hair died and varicose veins hidden and bright red lipstick; females with a jaunty gait and busts emphasized by opened shirts. Ah, fashions. The women of the capital were prepared to fight, to cut cane, to pray but always in style. They went to church or to the fields; they walked in the middle of the street, but always in style. Because in sixty three everything was new, different, progressive. They all forgot something, or someone, to be in Havana, near the *barbudos* and the hustle and bustle of the city. That year, for example, the cosmonaut, Pavel Popovich forgot the cosmos and shared the salt and heavy Havana air with Ann Lisa Tiesko, who forgot for a couple of days, the unions of Finland and shared posters and slogans with the anti–Franco Marcos Ana, who forgot, for several days, his struggles in Catalonia and Madrid to see the *barbudos* close up who were putting order to what was, by definition, disorder in itself. And among one and another, mostly the men, the voice of Benny Moré floated in the air who, in February, forgot how much he was needed in the world and was dying (the spoiled genius) leaving the bars and nightclubs in Havana flooded in tears and silence. And between the coffin of Benny and the cafeteria of the Habana Libre hotel where the poisoning would be carried out, noisy ANCHAR taxis drove by with their windshields covered with revolutionary stickers and stamps of the Virgin de la Caridad and the merchant boats that could not dock in Havana, while Polita Grau and Santos de la Caridad continued to wait, anxious, for the man who was going to be poisoned. But nothing doing. The ever-present, loquacious and elusive man was not showing up at the cafeteria of the Habana Libre. Everything was ready. The chocolate, the milk, the ice, the capsule, the hands of Santito but the man who was going to be poisoned only appeared on television, he was electrifying, delivered long speeches, waved his hands, and signed laws. Santito was despairing, whispering to himself from the great windows of the hotel that looked out toward Radiocentro,

> but you're right there,
> come to have some refreshment,
> you must be thirsty
> you've been talking for many hours,

now Santito moves away and looks at the TV and sees the man who was going to be poisoned, sweating, moving his hands, moving about in his seat. Santito thinks

> of the chocolate milk shake, cold and frothy…come on man,
> we're waiting for you,

but no way: not today either. The man who was going to be poisoned drinks water in front of the cameras, says good bye and, before leaving the building, behind the studio curtains he reads some international cables.

> *Adlai Stevenson announces another*
> *aggressive campaign against Cuba…*
> *France announces the explosion of its first*
> *hydrogen bomb in the Mangareva Islands, south*
> *of Tahiti…*
> *In Germany the Berlin Wall is sabotaged…*

he reads it all, devours it all, as if the enemy does not exist.

8

The hotel where the man who loved chocolate milk shakes was going to be poisoned had a short history in spite of its pompous inauguration in fifty eight. In a little less than a year, it had changed owners, and even worse still, had changed the name …

> but free from what

Polita complained who couldn't understand how that young man, who her uncle, Ramón Grau, the former president of the country, had known during the forties when he was merely a struggling lawyer of the Ortodoxo party, dared to play with politics. The nephew and niece of the old Grau, Mongo and Polita were disturbed by this. And very much together. Because of the «*grand barbudo*» Mongo Grau was no longer an important man, a fact that was surely upsetting; but the case of Polita was more serious. Polita had returned to the United States when Batista fell, enjoying the possibilities that opened up for her uncle (and, of course, for her) but, all of a sudden, she realized her mistake, all possessions were confiscated, years and years of work in the National Lottery gone to the winds,

how crazy, my God,

I'll no longer be able to stroll as the First Lady of the Republic, no longer the grand ostentatious lady with power, capable of taking care of her uncle's bachelorhood, the single Dr. Grau, she was a powerful woman, the *barbudos* had also gone against her and

that was intolerable.

It could be said that Mongo and Polita thought as one, remembering old times and they were decided to regain them. Thanks to her, "the old man", as the former president Grau was called by the people, had built highways, barrios, hospitals and had made the public accounts profitable, accounts of a country plundered by several sharks. Except him, of course: during his government she had been the only shark, his Polita. Doctor Grau was a decent physician, a veteran of the revolution against Machado, a man in the midst of bad company and poorly advised when he was president, betrayed by Prío Socarrás and by Chibás and by Batista and by the minister, Sánchez Arango and by the man who was going to be poisoned according to Polita's plans, the ever efficient Polita, always on the ball, strange and old fighter for democracy, a huge woman with specific weight and balls well placed although the masses thought of her as a big wheel like the shark who promoted what the people called the "bidé de Paulina"[4], that large fountain in front of the Sports Center as you drive along Boyeros. But, well, after all, what do the masses know, what do so many illiterates and followers of soapies know: nothing. Polita is too much woman for a country such as this. She can take it all, knows about all, water fountains and public funds, of the National Lottery, of the real estate of lands, of false revolutions and of orders given by the Church Commission, of chalets in Miramar and luxury hotels in

---

[4] The bidé de Paulina is a fountain that was popularly known as bidet of Paulina

Vedado. That is why, now, Polita doesn't understand why the Habana Hilton has been orphaned,
                    like taking the surname from a man,
she complained during nervous walks around Mongo,
                                        free from what, my God
and she tried to imagine the great Habana Hilton bound feet and hands, behind huge bars, a captive hotel that the *barbudos* wanted to liberate and give it a new owner,
                    ridiculous,
Polita and Mongo Grau were clear about that : the man who was going to be poisoned had gone crazy or took too seriously his role as a historical messiah. They often rode up and down along 23rd Street just for a sight of the big hotel and think, nostalgically, about the days they had spent there with their friends drinking brandy, beer, smoking Habanos and playing poker. Polita most of all. Almost every day she told her chauffeur that she was in no rush, and they headed to 23rd Street avoiding the noisy busses, the 64, the 10, the 22, the 32 or the 9, driving slowly along. She didn't look out at the scenery, or at the pedestrians, or the surroundings. Polita only had eyes for that hunk of a hotel, for its bright sign, adulterated, with a new surname and she repeated to herself, ad nauseam,
                    free from what, my God.
    The drive was, to say the least a curious drive. Since she crossed the 5th Avenue tunnel and went up Zapata to the Avenida de los Presidentes ("her Avenue"), Polita began to ooze adrenalin, her hands perspired until she crossed 23, turned off a bit further up and took to the main artery, La Rampa, always with a perfumed hankie in her hands and the dark glasses hiding her eyes,
    please slower,
she would tell her driver, and looked up at the floors of the hotel and yearned for the terrace in which she and Mongo and the unconditional followers had spent such good times. That drive was like therapy, later she had new strength to work on her historical mission: overthrow the man with the recently discovered gray hair. Not Mongo. Mongo also wanted to overthrow the man who was going to be poisoned but he was not given to the nostalgic drive along La Rampa. Mongo liked to go on foot, walk around the hotel, unnoticed among the people,

64

political perspicacity (Polita would say)
professional deformity (Mongo himself said)
wanting to take a stroll (his friends said simply)
but the truth of it was that Mongo Grau, at midday and two or three times a week had a "medianoche"[5] and an Hatuey, in the Carmelo of 23 and walked down La Rampa watching the people. He couldn't understand how a country could get so crazy. The so–called Revolutionary Government was picking couples living together and marrying them; it was sending the children (alone!) to the countryside; was filling Havana with *guajiros*[6], what a crazy thing, even the Habana Hilton was filling up with *guajiros*. This was really too much, pure show, demagoguery, political schizophrenia of the man who was going to be poisoned. Mongo Grau adjusted his glasses and whistled softly, as if lost in thought but his thoughts were far off, flying high. He knew that his sister, Polita, was involved in something big, that she had contacted with the Americans and had met in the Spanish Embassy with some people prepared to fight. His stroll was always the same. He left the Carmelo of 23 and went towards the Malecón[7], turned right on M toward 25 and went up turning along L towards Radiocentro and later went up 23 that had become the heart of this passionate youth. He would go the same route two, three times, looking at the hotel from different angles, the entrance, the side, the warehouses…A few times he went in, sat at the cafeteria to read Revolución, Hoy or Bohemia, a press filled with ominous paragraphs because they began to speak of Havana life in the past, to conjugate verbs with a suspicious accent, as if everything was irreversible. Nonetheless he read the dailies; he felt a pressing need to be informed of the changes. Most times he would leave Carmelo and walk, whistling, carrying a paper or magazine under his arm to read them later. Looking out from the terrace of the hotel, or even from the cafeteria, Mongo Grau was hard to identify. Another passer–by. That is why Santos de la Caridad, while he carefully put away the capsule of botulin Polita had given him, although he would look out the large glass pane windows once in a while and he couldn't

---

[5] A medianoche is a thick sandwich made with sweet bread coated with tomato sauce and mayonnaise and slices of ham, pork, cheese, and dill pickle.
[6] guajiro, the popular name given to the people who till the land.
[7] Malecón, seawall boulevard.

imagine that the elegant and slow man who circled the hotel so many times was Mongo. Also, for a man like Santito it was unthinkable that the nephew of a man who had been president and he, a simple waiter of the old Habana Hilton – it was difficult for Santito, Bartolomé and Saceiro to say they were workers of the Habana Libre; they referred to themselves as "workers of the former Habana Hilton". – could be involved in the same plan that, at the same time and a few feet from one another, were asking, …

when the hell will the man who was going to be poisoned come to the hotel?

A man like Santito only wanted to shake the milk and cocoa well and perfectly mask the presence of botulin, to win some points in the eyes of the previous owners of the hotel so that when they got back they would give him a promotion, improve their salary or make him, for example, the captain of some restaurant.

But, of course, Santito knew that Bartolmé García and José Saceiro, the captains of the two hotel restaurants also had botulin capsules and were waiting their opportunity. Polita had repeated tirelessly that

the Man eats and drinks
anywhere, where he finds himself
when he is hungry. The only thing to do was to wait
and be ready.

Each knew what he had to do and was convinced that it was easy. But Santito had a slight advantage: the man who was going to be poisoned was very fond of his milk shakes. Polita was clear, she said it clearly when she left the embassy she made the historical remark and using the tone of her enemies:

Comrades, the die is cast.

Now all that is left is to wait and not to worry: that was the strategy. The capsules had been put in a safe place and at hand when the man would appear. Santito felt that it would be him, something told him, it was a unique opportunity and this time he would not let it go. The day of the inauguration of the Habana Hilton, Batista had greeted all the workers when he had just gone to the warehouse. And twice, the very same Meyer Lansky and Santos Trafficante had been in the Casino and the Salón Caribe, but it was not his shift. Bad luck because with these "US businessmen" one never knows. Santito knew many who ended up working for them and were lined with dollars. Well, this would be his chance. No one better than him to do the job. Bartolomé and Saceiro said nothing but surely prayed that the man who was going to be poisoned would come hungry and not thirsty, when the day came. But, no way, they weren't smart or they were afraid, they had hidden the capsule too much. Santito knew that since this,

in an operation like this (this had been the exact phrase Polita used),

the most important was the swiftness and calmness and for that it was best to have the capsule within reach. But of course, he wasn't going to go about with it in his pocket, he was not going to put it on the bar, would not use a ring with a symbol embossed like in the Third Reich like the crimes against the Popes or the Caesars. No. In this case his strategy would be better. The capsule would always be in place, near the chocolate, the milk, the ice like another ingredient of a fresh drink. His capsule would be under the cafeteria freezer, well conserved and within reach without causing suspicion. When the day came he only had to take it, one only and logical motion: open the freezer and take it out at once, the ice, the milk, chocolate and the capsule. Perfect. This time it would be him. There was no doubt. Also, he knew that he, Santito, was liked by the man who was going to be poisoned. He rarely drank his milk shake without making some comment. Or he thanked him. Once he even gave him his hand. In other words, the man who was going to be poisoned, at least once, had shaken his hand, and when the time came he would take the capsule and mix it in with the ingredients and he would serve the milk shake.

9

When the man who was going to be poisoned took the glass of milk shake in his hands, at the very moment that he felt the chilled glass, the neighbors of the buildings in front of the hotel, on L street (all except the little boy in the second floor that had gone to the bathroom) were watching *San Nicolas del Peladero*[8], laughing at the dialogue between Agamenón and the Mayor's

[8] A very popular TV comedy about the wheeling and dealing of pre-revolutionary government politicians

67

wife and those living in the building on 23 and M, watching the same program except for three apartments: on 3 B where an old man was alone, a widower who was listening to Daniel Santos on the radio, in 2A where the couple were preparing congri [9] for supper, in 1C three couples were drinking rum and loudly arguing about their TV favorites, drunk, instead of watching San Nicolás del Peladero, praised Enrique Santiesteban and compared the program with El Show del Mediodia or poked fun at Casos y Cosas de Casa or told Enrique Arredondo jokes, some with a learned air, others gossiping about show biz as if living near Radiocentro gave them the right to speak of their favorite artists; they were knew Germán Pnielli, Rosita Fornés and Armando Bianchi, they felt like co–protagonists of each and every anecdote . In sixty three, everyone felt like a co–protagonist of something in Cuba, more so because they were televised. Before, only artists appeared on the air but now, thousands of Cubans appeared every time there was a demonstration, like a huge film super production. Let us not forget that Havana was the first capital in America to enjoy television, even before Washington and this transmission "precocity" and collective protagonists had given rise to television fever. That is why, among other things, the man who was going to be poisoned had transformed that small screen into a platform of political struggle, with long speeches, with the signing of laws, live, with direct trials… But television in sixty three was not in color nor did it use so many cameras, nor did it have simultaneity via satellite. That is why every one remembers the poisoning in black and white, and what is worse, in a straight line, as if those minutes had only been followed by events, not others, and exactly so, not any other way. Mistaken interpretation, of course.

When the man who was going to be poisoned took the glass of chocolate milk shake and brought it to his lips, smiling at Santos as he had done so often, the world didn't stop; none of the others took notice of that harmless gesture. The Havana taxis continued going up and down along 23rd and L Streets, in their Chevrolets, their Plymouths, their Fords, without noting the nervousness of Santito; in the University bus stop that used to be a streetcar stop, the passengers were restless over the delays of the buses without suspecting what was going on at the same time; those on the 64, 9, 32

[9] This is a typical food made rice and black beans

looked out their windows to the hotel, exactly towards the cafeteria, but did no perceive the danger; in the Salón Caribe, Norma Reyes honored the guitar, tensed her muscles and whirled all her curves around at the rhythm of the strings, to please the instrument; inside Cinerama, in front of the hotel several couples kissed holding hands, looking at *El esqueleto de la Señora Morales*, another story of poisoning, without suspecting that a few meters from the concave screen and the three cameras that gave a 3D effect, an identical action was under way, only in this case it was not Arturo de Córdova, the poison wasn't injected in an egg, the body wasn't hidden; here it was about the man who had discovered a gray hair, and the poison capsule had slept for weeks in the freezer and the body would be shown once the assassination was achieved, like a trophy in the Capitols of Havana and Washington. All this was happening, of course, in black and white. Rather in sepia tones. The man who was going to be poisoned arrived in sepia tones at the Habana Libre hotel crossing the lobby followed by his personal guard and other «poisoned» politicians; in sepia tones he greeted every one; in sepia tones he went to the cafeteria; in sepia tones Santos de la Caridad, the worried Santito, saw him come up to the counter and made comments in sepia tones to the others in sepia tones; in sepia tones Santito bid him Good evening and the man who was going to be poisoned told him

to serve him a cold shake;
please,

in sepia tones, Santito answered

with pleasure,

all in sepia tones and with very fast movements if we compare the scene reproduced now in television; yes, it was all in sepia tones, that is the true color of memory.

10

Santos de la Caridad was an experienced waiter, but knew very little about conspiracies. He had been chosen for the operation by Manolo Campanioni who, for his part, was guided by the Grau siblings who received instructions from William Harvey and Robert Maheu, but Santos didn't know anything about it. He didn't know, for example, who was John Roselli, one of the points of this network to kill the man who was going to be poisoned. John

Roselli was a well known member of the Cosa Nostra, a man with colts under his armpits, with his hat at an angle and dark ties, one of those men who have lost their face in films and have become part of the folklore of Chicago and Las Vegas, glamorous gangsterism. But, here and now, Roselli was a real, bone and flesh Mafiosi. Almost a year before the man who was going to be poisoned entered the cafeteria of the Habana Libre and drank the milk shake prepared by Santito, John Roselli had met with William Harvey in New York, who, at the time was head of the Project Rifle, one of the many plans to kill the man who was going to be poisoned. The contact for the meeting between Roselli and Harvey was one James O'Connell, who had also participated in the New York meeting, where everything began. At that meeting they talked for hours and smoked and drank and wrote down instructions in their own diaries; that was when the three capsules were shown, small weapons destined for Havana, one of which Santito had to put in the milk shake. Days later Harvey and Roselli met again, this time in Miami and Roselli said that he was in direct contact with Tony Varona, a really tough character, a guy who, in addition to «the little pills», also wanted weapons and radio equipment like in the Bay of Pigs. Harvey said yes to Roselli, there would be weapons and everything else, but they really weren't necessary, that those capsules worked

anywhere and against
anything, *man.*

Of course, neither Harvey nor Maheu nor Roselli nor even Tony Varona knew who Santito really was. Nor did Santito know that the capsule had come from so far away, from the Laboratories of Joseph Scheider. Separating Scheider and Harvey there was a whole world; between Harvey and Roselli another; between Roselli and Santito there were many people moving about: Tony Varona, Jaime Capdevilla (the attaché of the Spanish embassy), Polita Grau, Mongo Grau, Alberto Cruz, Manolo Campanioni …, even the other candidates to carry out the poisoning. Bartolomé Pérez García and José Saceiro. Bartolomé had been owner of the Bulnes and Gato Tuerto bars and now worked as a restaurant captain in the Habana Libre, a hurt businessman because the man who was going to be poisoned shut down his brothels. Bartolomé complained that first he had lost the business of the sailors (with the wailing of the prostitutes, with the suicide of a mulatta who claimed she was going to marry a Brazilian sailor) and that the majority of the whores had begun to study sewing…

where was that ever seen before? … how ridiculous that not even in Chinatown could Bartolomé find a source of money. The case of Saceiro was different, more like Santito: Saceiro missed the owners of the Habana Hilton and expected that with the poisoning he would gain points. They, too, did not know of Johnny Roselli. Well, the *Cosa Nostra*, yes, of the *Cosa Nostra* and its plans to share out Havana, yes they had coincided once with Santos Trafficante and Meyer Lansky in the Sans Souci Casino and in the Habana Hilton; but believed that this business of the capsules was the business of the Grau sibs(for political ambitions) and of the North Americans (for historical ambitions). The web was getting tangled. The Santos–Bartolomé – Saceiro triangle was clear. But the Polita – Capdevilla – Campanioni triangles was superimposed on the Roselli – Harvey – Varona triangle and all its angles, the hypotenuse was shrinking, the sides were getting longer and at the center of this spider web, the two sides of the obtuse angle, the side of the «chocolate milk shake» and the side of the «botulin capsule» both waiting for the arrival of the third side to close the triangle: the side of «the man who was going to be poisoned».

11

The man who was going to be poisoned had survived a number of different attempts of assassination, all discovered and broken up way before the planned actions by those who had only one mission, work, responsibility: to protect him. But something failed in this case. The time waited for by Santito for weeks. The man who was going to be poisoned was entering the appointed place, where everything was prepared, the chocolate, the milk, the ice, the lethal capsule, the hands of Santito… however, this time the Security team had not discovered anything. Three men of his personal guard went to the cafeteria with him, but they didn't know anything. It didn't happen in any plans with rifles with telescopic lenses, it didn't happen with the bazookas set up under a false roof in the eighth floor of the Misiones 29 in front of the Presidential Palace, nor with the plastic C–4 explosive that they would put in the sewer system under the platform where he would give a speech; nor with the plan to shoot him while he made a hit in the Cerro Stadium, nor with poisoned pens, nor underwater explosives, frog–men, the powders to make his voice squeaky during his speeches, the depilatory creams to have him lose his beard in public; something like this had never happened before, his personal guard had always discovered the conspiracies. But this time the plan had reached the peak without discovering anything; what's more, the time had come. There was the man. It was March 18, 1963. The night was warm and life was moving around the hotel, in sepia tones, but alive, several couples, holding hands in the Cinerama Radiocentro, watching Arturo de Córdova cleverly hiding the traces of the poisoning of his wife, Mrs. Morales, some in neighboring houses laughing with San Nicolás del Peladero; others are listening to the radio, others are setting the table and sitting down to eat (congri with chicken); others discussing about *Casino de la Alegría* and the horror of the Soviet films; the pedestrians and the bus passengers to up and down along 23, along L, along M, along 25, going around the hotel building but ignoring that the man who was going to be poisoned was walking towards the milk shake, slowly. Everything was ready, prepared. The man who was going to be poisoned wearing his military cap looser than other times. Santos sees him coming and swallows dryly,

give me a very cold
milk shake, please

and in sepia tones Santito answers,

with pleasure

and with the hands of an experienced bartender he approaches the refrigerator, with the hands of a budding conspirator, of an inexperienced poisoner. They are mechanical movements, fast and sure, the same movements of every day of every month for at least six years. The milk is fresh, in glass bottles. The chocolate is the best, from the last cargo from Minais Gerais. The sugar is native. The ice recently made. Santito then takes a tall glass with barely visible ridges, thinking that the man who was going to be poisoned would find the grasp stronger. Now the blender. A dash of salt, the exact amount that brings out the unequaled flavor of the milk shakes Santito prepares. And now the capsule. There it is; Santito and the capsule have waited days, weeks, for this moment; there is the capsule brought from the Joseph Scheider Laboratories; there it is, near the coil, waiting for Santito to take it in his hands and mix it into the delicious mix. Now Santito thinks that it would have been better if the occasion had been for his colleagues, Bartolomé or Saceiro. But there is no time. He slips his hand under the freezer, to the coil and touches the capsule. To his back he feels

72

the unmistakable voice of the man who was going to be poisoned and the laughter of some of his comrades. With his index finger he tries to loosen it, but he can't. The capsule is stuck to the coil with ice. Of course, no one had thought of that. With his thumb and index finger he tries again, he moves it a bit but nothing. Then he grabs it firmly, pulls it and something unexpected happened, something that had not been thought of by all the triangles; the capsule breaks. Because Santito may know a lot about mixing shakes and combinations of aromas and flavors but nothing about physics. Squeezing the surface of the partially frozen capsule it breaks in half and the poison spills along his fingers and the sides of the refrigerator. It's unbelievable. Santito trembles with astonishment, with anger, fear, disappointment, impotence, but no one notices. He looks around. He thinks of Saceiro, of Bartolomé, of Polita Grau, of Campanioni … He thinks of his bad star while a knot forms in his stomach and another strangles him. But Santito is a professional, let us not forget. So, in a few seconds the familiar sound of the Osterizer is heard in the cafeteria of the Habana Libre and the movements of the milk shake ingredients can be seen going up and down and around, the chocolate, milk, sugar, ice and that dash of salt that is his secret. A minute later, he pours it into the typical fourteen ounce glasses of the cafeteria; the man who was going to be poisoned, tastes his milk shake, offers his comrades in camaraderie and enjoys it to the last drop,

thank you very much, it was delicious

as always, and very fresh,

he puts the glass down on the counter and pulls down his cap, turns and leaves followed by his people. But before leaving the hotel he stops in front of one of the big mirrors of the lobby. The gray hair is still there, alone. Then he smoothes his beard to hide it a little and moves off in the long strides of a survivor.

Aguadulce, Almería, Spain, July 1, 2002

The CIA used the US Mafia to introduce the capsules of synthetic botulin in Cuba to assassinate Commandant Fidel Castro. This plan was research and acknowledged by the US Senate, in addition to seven others in 1975.

IT'S ME, MARIA If I am famous one day and could talk on the television I would like to tell the people that life is neither good nor bad, that it has good moments and bad ones and that is happiness, it can also be the wish to continue living, or the sadness that is the desire not to continue living but, although we could have gradually lost the good moments garnered in the years lived, it is still worth living, because there is still a chance to be happy and because there are many ways of being happy.

But, the truth is that life, sometimes, is vary unfair and absurd.

And to show you, listen to what I have to tell you.

It was the early seventies and, for us poor folk, life was a straight line and peaceful, like the barracuda when the sea is calm. It's true, there were problems but we didn't feel it because there was so much to do.

The boats were out fishing in international waters. Now we could put out to sea in peace and fish all we wanted because the boats were well fitted and were comfortable.

And, on the morning of May 2n^d, two boats went out to sea, the *Plataforma 1* and the *Plataforma 4,* bordering the banks of the Bahamas to fish *biajaibas* that were running with the moon. It was forty or fifty miles from Caiman lighthouse and they had to be out for six or seven days.

The kidnapping took place on the tenth day, just before turning back with the cold holds packed.

We heard about it the following Monday after someone heard on Radio Swan, during the soap opera program, the names of the fishermen jailed.

It was really something.

From the Torna family there was a father and son and a cousin, from the Del Rio family, two brothers and a cousin and five neighbors from the neighborhood.

People in Miami said that they wanted to exchange them for Vicente Méndez, who had disembarked in Oriente for sabotage operations and rise up in the mountains and who, in the end, was caught.

And this had never happened, neither before nor after the Revolution. No one could understand why they captured simple workers and they were kidnapped and treated roughly. All the laws were against this and, however, it was done. This was happening and it was happening to us.

And, it was about one in the afternoon, heaving to and after having a good meal of rice, chick peas and scrambled eggs with ham for lunch, the men were resting and trying to find what little shade there was, getting out of the sun that, at that time, was an oven.

They said that, all of a sudden, they heard motors approaching and when they looked out saw two speed boats. When they caught up with the boat they began to circle it while the crew took out all sorts of weapons. Then one of them shouted: "Lay anchor there if you don't want to go down …!" The first to lower anchor was the *Plataforma 4* and, a little more windward, the *Plataforma 1*. They ordered the captain to go to the prow and the crew to stay in the stern. Then they ordered to lower one of the lifeboats of the *Plataforma 1*, all get aboard and go the *Plataforma 4*. Then one of the speedboats approached and a man who appeared to be the chief said: "We are going to sink that boat, you're Castro's people, you're communists. If you give us trouble we'll sink you with the boat. That one we'll blow up right now."

Can you imagine such stupidity? The men were amazed and didn't know what to do. It seemed straight out of the films.

And then one of these guys boarded the *Plataforma 1*, fired a round of machine gun into the opening of the bunks. He went in and came out with a sack of rice that he threw overboard without saying a single word. Some wanted to protest but were shut up by the rest considering the danger they could face. Then another guy boarded the ship with a pack of dynamite and a long wick. There were about ten red cartridges, all taped together.

In the meantime the other boat was slowly sailing off.

When at about thirty meters away and with the explosive charge in place, the two guys jumped from the boats to the speed boat and went off. At about a hundred meters they started to shoot machine gun fire below the flotation line trying to blow it up but were unable to do it. Then they fired a bazooka and it didn't explode either. The explosion in the *Plataforma 1* was finally heard when the *Plataforma 4* was about a mile off.

Then they continued sailing for about two hours. The speedboats were at leeward and windward, always on the look out. A short while later, the one who was the boss ordered the motors shut off and two fishermen to move onto the speedboats. No one liked this at all. Nardo and Tavito decided to go and when they started climbing down they ordered them to take off their shirts and go down with their hands up, which was totally impossible to do. No one can go from one boat to another without holding on. That big was the terrible fear of these people. Once on the boats they were handcuffed. Then the rest of the crew was told to dismast the boat so that it could not be recognized as a Cuban fishing boat. The flag pole had to be cut down, throw the auxiliary refrigerator overboard, throw over the creel and cut the riggings.

When Nardo and Tavito came back on they said that they wanted to exchange them for the Vicente Méndez group that no one knew for sure who they were. They found out later that this Méndez had attempted to infiltrate himself in the eastern coast with a group and they were in prison. Of course, the boys did not understand anything, it was a matter for justice, of laws, and they were simple fishermen doing their work.

They continued to sail with the boat dismasted. A little later they ordered to lower anchor again. It was clear that they didn't know what they were going to do. Someone told them that they were going to blow up the boat with them on it and, of course, this wasn't funny at all.

After the scare they ordered to raise anchor and sail in the direction of a lobster boat that could be seen on the horizon, about a mile off. On approaching the fishing boat they changed direction again and sailed about fifty five degrees towards the Bahamas. They continued to sail until midnight.

They hadn't eaten anything and there were no signs that they were. Then they ordered to lower anchor and go to sleep.

About seven in the morning, and still without having eaten anything they ordered to start the motor and raise anchor. Then one of them asked if they knew Orange. The ordered to set sail north and they sailed until one in the afternoon when they sighted a lighthouse. At this time a speedboat approached that, at first they thought it was one of theirs, but what a to-do in the speedboats of the kidnappers; they thought there was something strange. Then the boys went under the deck in case there was a shoot out.

When the boat moved along side they could see that it is Ñiquito, the son of Ñico el Puto who was living in Miami and knew the boat and had come to visit. The kidnappers were talking aside with them, it seems that they scared them off and let them go. Ñiquito is the one who says in Miami that Cuban fishermen have been kidnapped and, through him, the news reaches Cuba.

Afterwards they continued to sail in the same direction and about a mile and half from the lighthouse they ordered to go south, to Orange, according to them.

About four in the afternoon we arrived at a key. By that time the boys had made a little condensed milk with water and hunger was a bit less.

They spent the night anchored near the key, feeling better because they were on land. They had some biscuits with canned meat.

When morning came, one of the speedboats took off.

About two in the afternoon a lobster boat flying an English flag shows up and there is a great commotion in the pirate launch. They tied on to *Plataforma 4* and boarded armed with two rifles saying that if they came to rescue them they would be killed. Can you imagine? Another scare. They had to say that they were submarine fishermen from Miami. That was a loony unbelievable story. One of the men jumped off and placed a magnetic mine on the boat so, if they were taken in, they would blow it up on the way to port. Another sign of cowardice from those people. It's like my grandmother used to say: they bought the head and took fright of the eyes.

At once they could see that it was a fishing boat and not a gunboat nor coast guard, nor anything like that. They were even towing five small boats and that's how it was and the men on the launch all scared.

After the English men left, about an hour later, a new launch arrived and they took Nardo again. They talked for about an hour and they came back with the order that they had to dock at a key. It was obvious that they wanted to get rid of the boat. They said they were from Alpha 66 and that the boys should collect their belongings and the food and get off on land. They weren't to be seen by planes nor should make any noise. They said they were in William key, Orange.

While on land they could see bundles of dynamite being moved to the boat. They wanted to blow it up and sink rapidly to the bottom of the sea.

Two men weighed anchor and began sailing looking for the southern coast of the key, anchored and the two guys boarded the speedboat.

Then they exploded the charge. The boat flew up but didn't sink. Then they decided to cut loose the anchor and let it drift off, let the current take it out to sea.

This must have been very sad for the boys. It was their boats with which they fed their children and worked under good conditions, good food and comforts. And it was uselessly being destroyed, disappearing, and they would never have it again. Another boat could be gotten but it wouldn't be the same. Whoever sails knows that, for the men, the boats are like family, like a strong and kind father who must be taken care of. And what hurt most was that it was being eliminated for no logical reason, no decency, no respect.

Since it was already late they began to cut down the underbrush with an old blunted mocha. A tent was made with the raincoats and their things were stored there.

The men on the launch continued to watch near the coast and with bad intentions.

Nighttime was difficult with the mosquitoes and gnats and then the cold set in that we did not expect. The boys set up two small boats against a crag and spread grass around. There they lay down and slept a bit.

At dawn they walked along the prickly pears to reach the coast without being seen from above. By mid morning they made a fire and warmed meat tins that they also ate with biscuits.

There they spent three days and three nights eating canned meat and combining them with other things taken from the boat until the food and water was used up.

The men on the launch would come down to land every once in a while and the boys found out that they were also out of food. There is a time when they proposed to them to attack a boat sailing by to take their water and food, but none passed. They were convinced that they had been tricked.

Finally, on the fourth morning the launch that had left first came back. On board were Nazario Sargen, Oscar Angulo and other men to interview the boys for the radio. Also with them was Guayo, the photographer.

They interviewed each one individually and asked the same question. How they had been treated and if they wanted to be exchanged for this Vicente Méndez. All said the same thing: that they had not been mistreated and wanted to return to Cuba, they didn't care if it was for an exchange, that they were not politically minded, and were simply workers. These interviews were later aired by Radio New York in the Radio Periódico Dominical program, the same program that gave the news that «naval units of Alpha had sunken two spy ships from Cuba and had captured eleven communists».

And that is what one doesn't understand about the Americans, how can the radio be used to broadcast news about those who are simply delinquents? Because behind all this was not only a political problem. Of course they wanted to kick up a fuss with the English and even blame them for the kidnapping and that is why they used Williams and Orange Key but the other reason was to prevent the Cubans from fishing off the Bahamas leaving the way clear for them to fish. Their intentions were to create fear and take their place. And what they were doing smelled of Mafia.

Then, after the interview they were told that they couldn't remain there, that they were going to be taken to one of their bases of operations where they would be better sheltered and taken care of.

About one in the afternoon and with a great show they boarded the speedboats and were taken from Williams's key, where the largest mosquitoes in the world were.

They went to the coast of Andros and anchored there around six in the afternoon in view of the island. There they slept as they could without food and water, nor anything.

The other day in the morning they laid anchor on the coast and ordered to take down their belongings quickly. They feared that a plane could sight them.

When Tavito was filling a barrel with water, Guayo told him: "Listen; there are some men from Alpha here with very strict orders so, if you don't behave, they'll do you in".

And it was true, five men and a launch remained about twenty five meters off with orders to shoot at night against anything that moved. They couldn't go out not even to urinate or have a shit. Everything had to be done where they could see us, during the day and later cover it up with sand to leave no trail.

Several days passed rationing a little food and water and waiting until it was all through. They asked the men on the launch for some and were told that nothing doing, no water or food. That simple. That it wasn't their responsibility. Again the same tension because there was nothing to do, just to remain calm, try to move as little as posible and wait. Hunger and thirst makes men drowsy and sometimes delirious and have strange dreams, and you're out of touch if this is reality or a dream.

One day, after many, they never knew how many, a new speedboat appeared. They laid anchor on the coast after circling a couple of times. Three men got off and one said they had news. What did the boys care about news? Water and food is what they needed.

After quenching their thirst, first with little sips to accommodate the stomach and later in gulps and, after eating something, they found out that the International Red Cross would be informed to pick them up and that it wasn't for cowardice, but that they acted through conscience.

That beats all, now they show up with this speech after several days almost dying of hunger and thirst.

They said they would leave food for a month and that no signal should be given after they left until the following day.

When they were leaving, the one who was boss said: "Guys, we are sorry for what has happened, but you help communism; God help you". And they took off.

At once they gathered some cans, food and water and began walking trying to get away from the area for fear the kidnappers would return. They went cutting down the scrubland because they didn't want to go along the beach to prevent leaving footprints.

It was around three o'clock when they started to walk. Some wanted to stay put. It hurt to walk barefoot among the tunas, the thorns and dogs tooth coral.

They halted at about seven at night, more or less. They all lay down to sleep while someone kept watch. About five in the morning they took off again. The idea was to keep moving to avoid getting caught again, always cutting their way along the scrubland and swamp.

At about nine they stopped and brewed coffee. They rested for about an hour and then opened some canned food.

Someone climbed a pine tree but couldn't see anything. They then agreed to return to the beach so they could be spotted by a plane.

Walking along the sandy beach, a light aircraft flew overhead but it seemed that the pilot hadn't seen them.

It was about twelve when they stopped to rest and eat something. Tavito went into the scrubland and came back with two long poles. He took off his shirt and after ripping it in half he made two flags that he tied to the poles and stuck them in the sand.

A short while later they spotted another plane flying low and they signaled it. Apparently he saw the flags because he circled around and flew over very low with a red cross painted in its underbelly.

After circling three more times they dropped a parachute with a package of concentrated food that was chocolate bars and tablets. There was also a message: "Don't move. You are rescued. International Red Cross".

Night set in without being rescued so they took to the scrubland for fear of being seen by the people from Miami.

The next day, around seven, back on the beach, they heard a loud noise and it was an amphibian helicopter that landed on the shore. They immediately asked about the group's health and if anyone was wounded. In truth the men were tired but no one was hurt, only with scratches from the bushes.

They took them off in groups of five. They arrived at an airport and an English representative and doctor received them. They were individually questioned, the doctor checked them and they later went to eat. It wasn't a full fledged meal, just the typical sandwich the Europeans eat and that we don't like because it has very little meat and a lot of vegetables and strange stuff. But for them it was glorious.

They were later told that Havana had been informed and that they would send a plane to pick them up.

After lunch they went to Nassau because the plane couldn't land in Andros. Later taking the Cubana plane and donning clean clothing, meeting with Fidel and the huge meeting in Havana.

82

There was a great commotion when the news reached the port. People would go from door to door and all took to the streets shouting with joy and gathered in the cooperative. The wives of the fishermen were taken to Havana to receive them. I even had to lend sandals, a skirt and blouse to Vergel's wife. Because she had nothing to wear and walked barefoot in the neighborhood. As if she was in the keys. I stayed with the four boys who were young. When she returned she had a bag with powder and perfume that they had given her in Havana and wanted to share it with me but I refused, it was like taking a new toy from a child. Actually, I knew how to use that stuff. And for her it was the first time and she wasn't used to it and felt that it was a great thing.

And Aida, Orosmán's wife, who couldn't go because she was advanced in her pregnancy they sent her a suitcase with baby clothing.

A few months later the captain of the Arigua found the sunken *Plataforma 1*, but in good shape. They managed to float it and sail again.

That is how the kidnapping ended. It backfired on them because the whole world heard of the injustice committed. And the families were the ones who suffered most, the mothers, wives and small children. My heart hurts from so much crying, Orosmán's little five year old girl told me and I thought: why does a little girl who should be playing with her dolls and play cooking, living the most beautiful time of her life, that is her innocence, why does she have to suffer and cry at such a tender age? It is not fair, life will give her moments of tears and sadness, but no one has any right to advance it.

For years, Cuban terrorists based in Florida, using gunboats have attacked fishing boats and kidnapped their crew.

THE MARK

It is not the pain that bites like a dog. Pain can be borne, pain passes. It is that desperation   inside and you have to learn to live with it. Some days it seems you can forget; your mind is busy and you feel like a normal person, like all the rest; but then someone arrives and looks at you, or you lie down to sleep and the old nightmare comes back; or you see a photograph in the newspaper and, there again, is the agony, the rage, the hatred tightening your chest. Sometimes it is worse. Things happen that bring it back. It is not even two months … In the afternoons I sit there by the window, with my embroidery, the people pass and greet me; sometimes they stop and buy something, or ask. I am at the window and I am a woman like so many others working for my living, honestly. Those are the good moments of the day. The children play in the street, a neighbor may stop and chat; one feels safe, calm, and happy, because that is happiness for me: to feel I belong to the place and the people around you, to give affection and receive it, a routine only interrupted by pleasant surprises. That is what I thought or did not with such detail, but I was calm and happy, one afternoon like so many others, scarcely two months ago, when the dog got loose. A Stanford. They train them to fight, I don't know how they do it; the owner lives at the other corner and we only hear the barks here; but everyone knows the dog is fierce, just as they know that he makes a lot of money with the fights, that are forbidden, but they do it just the same. They get used to seeing blood, suffering and the only thing they have on their minds is the money they are going to get, all they can buy with that money. The rest of the world doesn't mean anything to them. Well, what happened is that the dog got loose; they say he broke the fence and flew at the children. Can you imagine? He got the slowest one or the most frightened one, a little boy who was playing in the street with his friends, so innocent like he was sleeping in his bed; first the dog bit him in the arm and then he bit the leg. I saw it. I saw the teeth biting into the flesh and I felt cold, because that is the first thing you feel; a coldness of fear that becomes fire right away, a burning feeling and such great pain that you can't even scream. The bite of a furious dog. He would have ripped the boy apart if the people hadn't run and beat him off with a club; they had to leave it unconscious to free the child. They picked him up and ran to stop a car. They passed by here and I saw the wounds, the black flesh, the drops of blood; I heard the screams, theirs, mine were bursting inside, exploding in my head; my hands swelled so much from grasping the bars of the window so strongly; because I couldn't run, I couldn't carry the boy; the only thing I could do was look and feel a terrible agony. I saw the dog's owner pick it up and carry it off under the shouts and threats of the people. I waited for the return of the people who took the child. They had left him in observation and the parents were with him. Everything returned to normal gradually; but I have felt despair as the days pass, the same as what I felt then. Because I simply cannot accept it. Now the boy is playing in the street again, he's got scars, but they will begin to disappear with time; he was lucky. The dog's owner went to trial, paid a fine and now has the dog on a chain and wearing a muzzle. But, when he considers the dog recovered he will fight him again. He has to be careful in the barrio; they say he gave the boy a crate of malt refreshment. There are those who excuse him. But, I ask: who trained the dog? Who taught him to be a killer? Who gave him a treat when he tore another to pieces? I turn my head every time he walks by. Others can forgive; say that so much time has passed. In my case, years have passed and they were not dogs blindly attacking but, also, trained to kill and expecting their reward. In the hospital someone told my mother, trying to console her: "God did not want your daughter to die". And, mother, in desperation, shouted "And did He want her to lose her foot?" And the person who spoke to her added: "Think that she could have died, accept it". My mother didn't answer and I didn't even know who was talking but the words were engraved in my mind forever because, many times, I was told the same thing, perhaps a bit differently. And, I don't want to think that I could have died. Quite the contrary, I could have lived like a normal girl, running, skipping rope, use high heels, dance at my fifteenth birthday… I could have done all that, I should have done it and they didn't let me. I didn't have polio nor was I run over by a car, those things that perhaps we don't know who to blame. But, I am sure who the guilty ones are. That is why forgetting is not possible; simply push the memories back for a while. Of course, you are not going to be bitter and ruin the life for the rest of the people around you. You'll reconcile yourself with your lot, you pretend that you would have wanted to be a singer and that you don't have the voice, you seek refuge in embroidering and sitting at the window but, although you don't say it, you always carry the mark inside, deeper than the scar of the stump that no longer upsets me. Because the worse is not the pain, it's the desperation that is left inside of you.

On October 12, 1971, in the evening hours, a group of terrorists in an armed speedboat from Florida attacked the hamlet of Boca de Sarná in Banes, Oriente province. Two persons were killed and several were wounded, two of which were minors, Nancy and Angela Pavón, 15 and 13 years of age, respectively. One heavy caliber bullet ripped Angela's foot and had to be amputated.

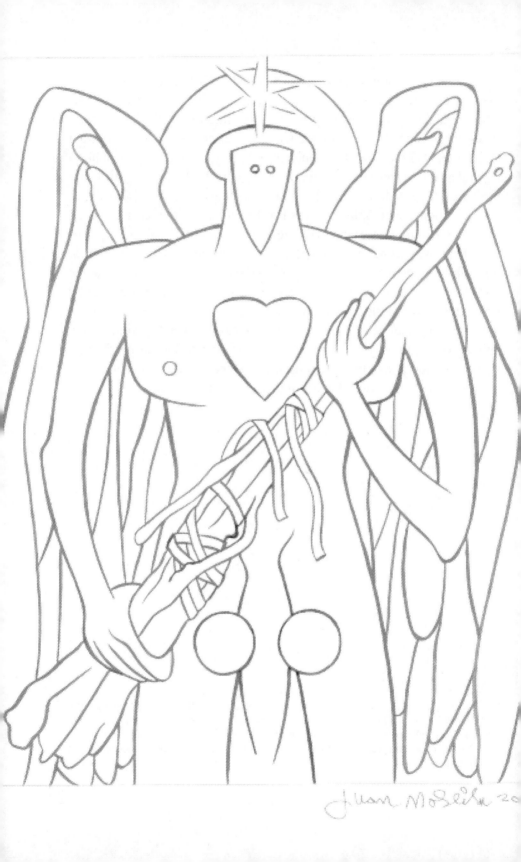

CAMERA FOCUS Before I used to drink; at times, without any special interest, without an effort to erase the surroundings of my existence. I was aware of the limit, that's true, difficult in any kind of vice. I drank until I reached unreality; to rid myself of disagreeable missions until, without sorrow, persecute the protesters through the dark streets, who caused too much trouble. After a drink nothing was punishable, orders were orders; after all, one had to keep calm and do well anything that had to be done. Alcohol set me apart, made a cut between my physical and spiritual being. The spiritual me did not consider consequences or charges against it and thus, many times, achieved total calm. But persecution depresses if you have a rifle, trained men and, the pursued, on the other hand, is not an odious person but a woman with pointed breasts Sophia Loren's face; or a youth with football player's legs, jungle hair; or a child, yes, still young, who go against the established order, against the power, who conspires with the woman and the football player, scattering pamphlets, writing on the walls, participating in disturbances. Persecution under these conditions is good for insomnia because the faces start to look like those of your nephews, your children or yours when you were that age. For these guilty feelings a stiff whisky, tequila, rum is good until, after half a bottle, you stop feeling. Others don't need it; they can look on a pile of bodies and sleep a heavenly sleep as if they are watching a film scene.

I still need to blot out images with whisky, blot the memory of myself thirty years ago, in uniform, strong, the bastard, although true to form; already with the flask of Johnny Walker that he takes out when no one is looking and the liquor touches his lips, deliciously. It is still necessary to blot out the handsome man for whom so many women sigh openly; it is necessary to blot out the envy of other policemen because those who open up are a dime a dozen and he does not forgive, he leaves them wet, perverted, who bite at his uniform, who betray their husbands, crazy, fearless, he leaves them being faithful to him, his hairy chest, his black eyes and his inexhaustible nerve. It must be blotted out but that me is obstinate. His men see him come and smile. They respect him, of course. That me is a stalwart officer who, at the same time, respects the colonels and generals and today, precisely, he took a drink in the bathroom to relax because he has a very secret mission, historical. I would like to avoid that image, to move away from that past again, but the General calls on the telephone, his voice is engraved in my memory, he speaks to my me. "All are here, my General", I answer. "Yes General my men have been warned. Of course, my General". And I go to the hall... The intellectuals are talking with animation. My men, disciplined, alert. I guess who are going to be the authors of the very secret attack among the intellectuals present. No one had described them to me. No one had given me a clue on how to find them, where they would be posted. The General with dark glasses gave brief information: "Two men are going to kill the bearded man; you have to prevent their falling into the wrong hands". And I said: "Don't worry, my General". Now it amuses me to discover the cunning ones, how ridiculous, making believe they are not what they are, how ridiculous, historical and secretive. Different to the other reporters, they ask no questions nor take notes; they aren't interest in what is being talked about; they look like children playing at being cameramen, kids receiving elementary lessons on how to behave like adults. One is tall, gray haired, uses glasses; the other, a mestizo, of curly hair, of average height. They move from one place to another, uneasy. Many change angles, too much for a simple television program. Anyone could have spotted them; they only needed to know what was going to happen. Now, if someone is up in the clouds, of course, they cannot distinguish between an American

90

ranger and an old woman with a cane. My me, however, is on the ball, because he is not only handsome and respectable, but also, astute and is aware who is what he looks like and who isn't.

A large round of applause when the objective makes his entrance. The future authors of the attack approach him, at an infallible distance. Of course, there is a barrier, a stop, a red sash. The objective is guarded by the gods. There, in Africa, certain shamans have prepared him the strongest talisman any mortal could have. Thetis held the small Achilles by the heel while she sunk him in the river. For this one, the Black witch doctors have protected him to the last hair of his beard and his compatriots, Caribbeans all, are hypnotized, they excitedly applaud every phrase, every pause, every gesture. The dove that once rested on his shoulder, without any prompting, was an African saint that had changed into a dove to proclaim his alliance to this man. That speech was just an excuse to demonstrate it. Later, no one has been able to break the myth. Problems of the Blacks, some would say, but even his enemies are impressed. This same gray haired man, I now realize, has followed him everywhere without daring to open fire. What stops him? The same thing in the embassy that, five days ago, in the San Miguel Commune, he was with his camera, eating shit as if he were a real reporter of Vene–Vision and not the man hired to assassinate a president. Would the gray haired man consider the outcome, in the importance of his life, in the possibility that the Chilean police may leave it to chance once the firing starts? In this situation, you are a soldier and, even without thinking of a posthumous glory, it is a luxury; and you have to be prepared to kill or be killed for a cause. However, a well-paid soldier is never a good soldier. Although all, at one time or other, are prepared to die for something or someone – I myself am capable of dying for my children – no one risks ones skin beyond certain limits. The person who has the vocation of an assassin, who accepts eliminating a human being for, let us say, half a million dollars and, consequently – if the victim is important – gain fame, is different than a true soldier. Both bear arms, both are prepared to use them, both follow orders. The real soldier, however, acts in a firm faith, like the one that convinced Abraham to sacrifice his son. The assassin needs to survive the mission to enjoy the pay. Is the gray haired man thinking of his own destiny, on what would happen after eliminating the man that so many people think invulnerable? It is a strategic mistake to think of the future because, far from being a philosopher, the gray haired man is one who fights for democracy, a man who gave his word, who said, yes, I'll shoot, I've got the balls, I am and no one else, in the name of all who fight, the one who is going to kill the villain; but, apparently, he has already seen himself prematurely covered in glory and I think, that he should leave off so much shitty daydreaming and pull the trigger and let the bullets splinter the lens of the sub machine gun and penetrate the thorax of the victim.

Time is in his favor, it's true. The objective, standing up, index finger pointing up, speaks of Yankee imperialism, he lengthens his answers, talks of Chile, of the bright road it is going to take. The gray haired man prepares the focus with the calmness of an old angler. Then, for the first time, I discover the shadow that moves among the public with the speed of a gazelle and falls on the gray haired man. For a moment, he lowers the camera and the shadow disappears. No one is worried. All are intent on the answers of the objective, ignoring the gray haired man, his intentions, me, wanting a drink. Then I decide to ignore the event, believe the apparition a sign of the nervousness I have lived with these days and I concentrate on checking out my men, in observing them until the gray haired man again lifts the camera at less than ten meters from the objective.

Those who have prepared the attack don't have the same courage or the same cold blood to defy the bodyguards. One of the organizers – a Mr. Veciana, I believe – was a smooth talker, with energy perhaps, but from a comfortable position, there protected by the Americans with his diplomatic post in Bolivia, earning good money at the cost of others who do get their feet wet. Dream, of course, sure he dreams of assassinating his enemy, of filling him with lead and later receive the ovation from the public; but from the dream to the act the balls of the gray haired man are needed. The other, the mestizo, doesn't count. With all his background of having placed bombs in a Polish ship, he is totally dependent, scared out of his wits. The initiative depends on his accomplice. Actually, both have few chances of coming out untouched. The bodyguards are skilled, they can place a bullet through the eye of a needle and that offers an advantage because they can drill holes in the intestines of anyone who makes a suspicious move because they protect, with their broad chests, the life of their boss and won't let anyone kill him nor stay alive if they try.

The gray haired man simulates a panning with the camera viewing the front rows. Some pose. In the meantime, the objective continues answering questions of the journalists and always, in a miraculous turn, accusing the Americans of sabotages, slanders, economic blockade. He amazes the public. He jokes between paragraphs. Laughter is heard. There is an environment of well being unfavorable for any attack. The gray haired man also makes a smirk that doesn't quite look like a smile, more like an ass kisser, I would say. The objective looks like a predicator; the rest, imbeciles letting their brains be washed at the Marxist fountain. When the shooting starts, my men will maintain indifference, with the chests on the floor until the shooting stops. The General has been explicit:

– After they kill the bearded man, the men will surrender.

Any moment now the action should begin, it is dangerous to delay it. The police may believe that, again, nothing will happen this time and, then they will be taken unawares. I really believe that the mestizo who cannot control his fears may shut his eyes, shoot wildly at the mass of people, and kill everyone but the one that has to die. For the second time the gray haired man lowers the camera, talks to his accomplice. I don't really care about the outcome. If the agents come out alive, all well and good, I capture them and then let them escape. If they die, its better. It seems that it is better for them to die, to fall in combat. There is probably a false file ready, photographs, identifications, letters, that link them to Russian spies and the Cuban Secret Service. The Americans know how to do that. Anyway, I insist, I couldn't care less what happens. I couldn't care less about the gray haired man, the mestizo, the witchcraft.

The third time the gray haired man focuses again, I have no doubt he will fire. The mestizo holds the camera at waist height, ready to give support. The gray haired man has the determination of a real soldier, there is no more holding back, the lead is going to burst, there the hero, there tomorrow in the press reports, there in Miami celebrating, champagne, there the turn in the future, there, my land, there, nothing the same as of today, the hell with it, a shiver, there, it can't be, not that way, **NOOOO**. The shadow has appeared again and covers the body of the gray haired man, something serious is happening, I know now, I always knew. No one reacts to the apparition, no one looks at it. I keep calm. The shadow wavers above the man and he makes a last effort, he manages to separate his feet, to over-come the surprising shudders; there it goes, the homicidal camera, there it goes, ratatata, he'll kill a handful of Marxists and their chief, ratatata. Miami joyful, wide coverage, champagne. I look for the body that projects the wavering silhouette. Obviously, it must come from above, I think. There are only lights there, only the whiteness of the ceiling. The objective made an-other joke. The journalists laugh again. The objective is still standing, offer-ing his entire body for the shot. I look at the gray haired man again. The shadow now, incredible, has transformed into something sharp, a sword perhaps. I rub my eyes, scratch my head but my sight insists on seeing that unique gray cloud. I think it is an optical illusion, a play of lights, a freak of the secret, historical command. Ready to fall to the floor, I place my hand on the cartridge belt, I tighten my teeth, muscles tense, here it comes, here it comes, the shots should burst, wounding the chest of the objective and then death rattles, screeches, broken glasses and chairs, running about, scream-ing, horrified, get this you son of a bitch, ratatata, aaah. But nothing hap-pens, the laugh of the objective is still there, the journalists, and the shadow digs deep into the belly of the gray haired man, applause, it disappears inside him, applause, it comes out and again digs in and comes out again, applause, until the gray haired man doubles up, closes his eyes in pain, applause.

At no time did the objective look at the mestizo and he, as ruled by a strange force, points his camera on me and, by pure instinct, I hide behind one of my men. The gray haired man feels his belly. He looks weak, terri-fied. He talks with his accomplice who says nothing. The gray haired man, undoubtedly, doesn't care if he is offended, he wants to leave, to flee. Both leave. Finally, they get out of the place by one of the side doors. I'll never see them again, only remember them from time to time, most of all when I stop, like now to watch the shadows of the clouds over the plains.

I am a different me, an old soldier enjoying his retirement in the easy chair of the country house, a guy with time on his hands who last week, purely by chance, had a book in his hands where he read:

[…] in 1971 Fidel Castro visited Chile. There, his assassination was planed to happen at a press conference on December 3. Purely by chance he escaped unharmed.

94

I believe this paragraph was written with extraordinary frankness. More so because after leaving the hall, the gray haired man was operated on in an emergency, allegedly suffering an appendicitis attack and many believed he had gone crazy when he ripped off the stitches of his wound and, with his own hands, opened it and, in his bloody pajamas, asked to remain in hospital. Yes, extraordinary frankness because the book narrates other failed attacks, failed by "pure coincidence". So much proof, even against the faith I practice, against the better judgment that should typify a career soldier, I have come to believe that the shadow stabbed the gray haired man repeatedly; it was not an illusion due to my exhaustion, nor the effects of whisky or a simple play of lights. It seems unlikely, I know, more so because I am the only witness of that event. However, why doubt that there are others, who fear to be laughed at publicly, who kept quiet just like me, until today.

Santiago de Chile, June 2002

During the visit of the Cuban president to Chile in 1971, terrorists of Cuban origin, residents in the United States, planned to assassinate him.

m y l e n e   f e r n á n d e z

THE GHOSTS

—Carolina's parents say that we are shitty Cubans – and with that phrase, she swings and thinks of how adult she sounded using that word, shielded by simply being a five-year-old messenger.

We're at the place of confessions, the fourth column from right to left if you stand facing what seems to be a sort of Greek temple that has a ping pong table. When we are not trying to learn the game, it collects the dry grape leaves that hang from the roof, those grapes that – after tasting them for the first time, marveling that they really do exist and not only in picture postcards or cartoons in Havana – are an enjoyable fruit and some magazines.

The place for confessions is in the patio in our house that is in the barrio that is in Santiago de Chile. In this barrio of little houses of the song by Victor Jara, everyone complains of the shortages, the black market, the disturbances, the strikes, the changes that have been occurring for some time now, a time that continues onto the winter of 1973.

—Here, we also talk about Carolina's parents – I tell her to help her understand that we are not the only ones judged.

—Yes, Bertha says that they are *momios* and that they don't want us in this neighborhood because we are communists like the Russians in the corner.

We only knew the Russians in the corner by sight. They lived in a dull white house and they were blond like the protagonists we saw in the Riviera cinema on Sundays. We just see them go in and out of the house and car. They are always serious. They don't talk to anyone, no one talks to them. Like us if we hadn't known Carolina in this same place.

One sunny morning, towards the end of last winter – a season that filled us with wonder, almost whimsically thinking about August in Cuba, where everyone was at the beach while we added wood to the living room's fireplace and told horror stories livened by the ghostly images of the flames –; we were bored of moving about the house and drawing, reading, watching Mexican soap operas, playing with the toys, the cuddly toys, with candies, with nothing, with memories. We hung to that first ray of sun and went out into the patio. That star that timidly sent its first rays as if asking permission not wanting to disturb, a clear, clean and subtle light. Happily we bundled up to the ears with those clothing that at first made us laugh seeing ourselves and then seeing both in the mirror. We looked fat, like two round and clumsy *push and backs*, but we were now used to them and were even able to jump in quickly and change amazed laughter for intrigue.

We went out and looked at the sky and at the sun to take it in completely – *Padre Sol* was the song by Tormenta that was in the hit parade and his *deja que venga el sol otra vez y después nos iremos con él[1]*, the *chic* verse that always came to mind – to remember it when, a half hour later, after it had gone down hurried by winter, the cold air and clouds that claimed there calendar right to hover over the city and our patio.

We went to hide behind the fourth column of the temple to escape from Bertha, to avoid hearing her bossy voice always reminding us that the beds weren't made or the toys weren't picked up or, even worse, her call to lunch and the fearsome and unfailing asparagus. We couldn't manage to change them, neither with mountains of mayonnaise or bread and butter. Cascades of soft drink couldn't drown them out in our throats and hide their taste. Nothing. Bertha said they were good, nourishing and this inevitable decision made them part of the menu for many lunches and dinners.

[1] *let the sun come again and then we will run after it*

We crouched low covered by the column and the leaves feeling completely hidden, almost invisible that made us laugh nervously, that laughter that comes when you know you shouldn't laugh and that makes you laugh even more and, in crescendo, until the head of Carolina appeared over the wall and her eyes, mouth and hair laughed with us. We signaled to her conspiratorially and accepting our invitation, she jumped over the wall.

That way, whispering, enjoying the pleasure of conspirators, we found out that she was eight years old, that her father was a dentist with an office in the Avenida de los Leones and that her mother had a boutique at home, always with articles from Paris. That now things weren't good with this government and if they continued this way they would lose everything and be poor.

She had seen us move in, knew the previous tenants – two girls like us who now live in the United States and whose father was taking a course in Medicine – she knew we were Cubans and were going to a school only for Cubans and the three of us had so many questions and answers to build a bond of friendship.

– But Carolina is our friend – Lili battles again, lifting her up like a great treasure, supported by the irrefutable fact that she saw her first.

– Yes she is, and very nice, she reminds me of Niurka who always ate mandarins...

– So why does her mother bang pots and pans?

– Because her mother is not our friend. At least she doesn't do it in front of our house like the others who surely think that it is our fault that they are going to go hungry.

La derecha tiene dos ollitas, una chiquitita y otra grandecita. La grandecita la tiene muy llenita, con pollo sin papitas asado en cazuelita. La chiquitita se la acaba de comprar; ésa la usa tan sólo pa'golpear... [2]

This song by the Unidad Popular became our exorcism against the constant banging and the great concert in front of our house, a great metal symphony, a chorus of women's voices that we watched from our room. The first day, Bertha and our mother took us out of the room and took us to the small

[2] *The right has two pans, one small and one bigger. The big one is very full with chicken without potatoes, roasted in the pan. The little one she has just bought for the only purpose of banging on it...*

television room to watch *Sombras tenebrosas*, trying to scare one fear with another. Other times, Bertha, decided as always and without paying any heed, closed with a bang the shutters of the door that opened up onto the terrace, the garden and the gate from where the noise came. Then she played with us, tickled us and called us *bambinas*, because the current soap opera was called *Muchacha italiana viene a casarse* and the Italian girl who was coming to get married sometimes said words in Italian. At other times, she told us of her town: Temuco, in an agricultural region to the south of Santiago where the Mapuche[3] farmers were trying to recover their lands. One day she began to teach us the song. We were no longer afraid. When the pots and pans began to sound, we closed the shutters and both of us cuddled in my bed and we sing very low, like a salm, a pray to St Johns Bosco, a wish sent to the fairy of Pinocchio or of wonderful thoughts to go to Never never land.

When Bertha found out of our friendship with Carolina she got very angry. We lived under the conviction that everything was risky and people more so, although we were only eight years old. But, behind that look of a quiet Indian, there was much space for laughter and Carolina found, in our house, an enjoyable friend with her bossy manners and her inflexibility on making us eat asparagus. She was a sort of mid way between two child-hoods, two forms of speaking Spanish and two ways of having tea.

- And if I tell you about something I did, will you challenge me?

Lili's Spanish had gotten a bit lost in the midst of new words to speak the same language. Her accent was absolutely "*del Mapocho*" and she often confused things. She didn't understand what was happening, why our father came home so late, why our mother didn't laugh as much as she did in Havana, why we couldn't go out to play and why the school bus waited in front of the house until Bertha opened the door and greeted the driver. I was the "older sister" and the one in charge of explaining things to her.

- What have you done this time?

Her last ruse was in a shop where we bought snow boots to go to Portillo for the weekend. The shop girl asked where we were from and my father said Venezuela. Lili opened her mouth about to correct the answer although

---

[3] Araucanian-speaking South American Indians_

she didn't manage to get the words out because I covered her lips with my hands, how they would do to Donald Duck and told her, it's a game. I'll tell you about it in the car.

The story was simple and covered just about all of us, like the truly important things. We had bet that we could imitate other American accents; she didn't stop talking because she sounded like a real Chilean. A bit sad for being left out of the game; she promised to keep quiet in the future.

- I have told her about the ghosts. But, she promised not to tell anyone.

They have lived in the house for a long time but at the beginning we weren't aware because their spells were always directed elsewhere. They were most fascinated by my parents' room and did their mischief without our noticing. Later they decided to try their magic in our room and so the ghost became a family affair, a daily comment, charms and surprises every day.

Like all ghosts, they were unpredictable. Some times, they were hard workers like in some of the stories of the Grimm brothers, and you could imagine them around the house doing good things for us. Returning home, we were surprised to see our beds made, the clothing and shoes picked up and the toys in their place. Some times, they left flowers for my mother with small cards but she did not love them. They made her nervous, she would glance around as if making a first check of the damages after an accident and she hugged us tightly, with no space between our bodies for even a little ghost to squeeze in.

When they moved into our space, they were tender, like good children and orderly doing things that would please our mother and Bertha as if we had done them. They tied bows around the necks of the cuddly toys; made our beds knowing that Lili slept with a light brown bear and mine was dark red; they hung up the clothing and gathered the dirty clothes in the wash basket; they organized the books; threw candy wrappers away that we kept in the drawer of the night table and wrote on the mirror; with adult letters, like those who want to please the little ones: "Hello girls".

But, some times they were angry. They overturned the blankets, threw the pillows on the floor, emptied the drawers on the rugs and threw the dolls into a pile of ears, legs, heads and tails. I explained to Lili that they did not always agree with everything; they had their small battles and used our room for their disputes, our things served as shelters and barricades. It wasn't "with" or "against" us; it was just "their business". She cried over the mischief of the ghosts, my mother and Bertha picked up the room without a comment and I felt that there was danger, that chance didn't stop with the banging of the pots and pans on the other side of the gate.

– We live in a bewitched house, like the one of Barnabas Collins – I told her the day of the disappearance of the photograph of us building our first snowman –, they need the photographs to see our faces well, like in the picture in the house of Barnabas – and I again quoted the US series that had everyone on tenterhooks, fearful and fascinated in front of the television every evening at nine.

One day my father commented in passing, in jest, as if it were not important, that we would probably never take photographs in the mountains because the cameras disappeared the Monday following the excursion. Another comment was that "they" had good taste in music because they played Dylan singing to the walls and furniture until our return, always after we went out. They smoked tobaccos, drank rum and when we returned home the ice melted in the glasses with half of the rum, the tobaccos burning in the ashtrays and Sinatra singing to the strangers in the night. The only thing missing were the ghosts.

Days of wine and roses by which the house received us, with the table decorated with flowers and expensive wines and, in our room, tempting boxes of chocolate bonbons and my mother and Bertha flew into the room immediately while I explained to Lili that if we ate them we would become ghosts and would never see our parents again; we wouldn't be able to return to Havana nor see our grandparents, our friends and we couldn't even play with Carolina; we would always be little and would have to live hiding and doing mischief in the houses of other people. She looked longingly at the chocolates and got a promise from Bertha, who always had a soft spot for *la piccolina,* that she would buy her those stupid sweets that weren't nourishing and quenches your appetite and prevents you from eating what was really important. She promised to buy them the next time she went to the market.

– I won't stop you from telling Carolina about the ghosts if she promises not to tell anyone, but how can you be sure she'll keep quiet.

– Because they have asked her in school about us, and she has answered that she doesn't know us.

– Are you there? – I asked my mother one night, unable to sleep. I looked out the window and saw the blue car, parked a few meters from the entrance, like so many other nights, so many other nights that they stayed in front and we provoking them keeping them awake.

My mother answered silently. Sitting in bed looking at the wall and, perhaps through it, about the time in this troubled city where the minutes count and one never knows for whom; where every day dawns with great differences and the ignorance of some; the certainty of others and the uncertainty of everyone controlling all the clocks of the inhabitants and the hopes of the country.

I returned to my room and thought that, perhaps it would be better for the ghosts not to know about Carolina. I got in Lili's bed and kissed her. I'm cold, I said to justify the fact that I only feel sufficiently protected by her closeness and her absolute innocence of everything we are living through.

It is a Monday morning in winter. Santiago continues with its daily disruptions of these past weeks. Striking by truck drivers, business persons, physicians, vandalism in daylight, those that have become an almost common spectacle where the "lolos"[4] break windows, set up bonfires, stop traffic and shout that Chile continues to be a free country. The police respond with tear gas and water hoses. The students demonstrate on the streets and chant: "Stop a civil war".

We have witnessed a shooting with the Patria y Libertad a few weeks ago. We protected ourselves from the gases returning rapidly to the movie theater from which we had left five minutes ago, the last time we went with Bertha and Carolina to see Fantasia.

Like any other day. That's what the streets are now in the city. But, today I am not frightened, perhaps because I'm a little girl, because it is daytime and I think that nothing can happen to us with so many people about. Because my father is at the wheel and we have closed the windows

---

[4] A local expression referring to young people between the ages of fourteen to twenty one (Editor's note)

to avoid the water, the gases, and the shouts. Because I think that our heads are protected under the metal roof of the car, now battered with coins thrown from the buildings of this avenue filled with offices and shops in answer to the slogans of the left. Because there are police, the embassy, my grandparents in Havana and the book by Dickens on the night table with the book mark in David Copperfield who escaped the boarding school to find his aunt.

The policeman stops us. The streets have changed directions and routes immediately; we must take another route.

But that is not what this man says. He talks of the car's license plates, the name of my father, and the address of our home. He speaks the words attack, bomb and offers to escort us there.

This place we had left so recently and that is no more. The street entrance is cordoned off; the police try to move the curious back. The neighbors gather around, they talk, move their heads, move off. The wall of the garden is intact. It still supports the gate and the door and the garden shrubbery at the entrance giving a false note to the house.

I can't see much. People, voices, gray sky. I think I can still smell smoke but I don't know if it is real or if I'm seeing those lightening images where things happen and later, you remember them all your life and the memories cannot put them in order.

I don't know if I got to see the house in ruins or invented the balconies crumbled in the grass that bordered the small stairs that led to the entrance door that now leaned on the stair grinding the wood that, at the end of the hall, rose to another floor. On the grass in a mountain of objects were a part of our lives. If it was Carolina who was making signs at me and shouting something I couldn't hear and those were her last words to me.

They took us away in one of the embassy cars. I had only one fixed idea, holding the hand of Lili, that I had to take care of her, that I owed her some words. She did not cry and her hand, that did not shudder, gave me strength and a certain security which, unexpectedly, reached us in the midst of chaos and terror.

Santiago stormy, as if the explosion in our house had moved the city that, even in times of peace, moved uneasily, disturbed by the earth tremors. We get out of there, of our parents and the scenario of the last two years of life. I look through the window at the passing scenes like nervous film clips of the corners, trees, pedestrians.

Radio Pudahuel gives the news, that it is us and gives our now non exis-
tent address and the phrase: "terrorist attack". And, Lili listens wide eyed as
if, instead of words, what comes from the radio creates images, a series of
vignettes that take on a third dimension. She listens with her five years of
age that now seem to be raising up, stretching and first receiving surprise,
later amazement and, finally, the conviction that the ghosts wouldn't do something like this.

In August of 1973, days before the coup d'état against President Salvador Allende, a bomb
exploded in the residence of the commercial attaché of the Cuban Embassy in Santiago de
Chile where his wife and two daughters also lived. The eldest, who had 10 years at the time,
is the author of this story.

To Betina Palenzuela Corcho,
her father and brothers

BETINA'S MONOLOG

I have always thought[1] that I could have been different, perhaps happier, less responsible. In the short time with her my mother taught me to be that way. I was too young when that happened…How could I be carefree and happy-go-lucky like the rest of my schoolmates after such a monstrosity? An adolescent who loses her mother at the age of twelve, a mother destroyed by a bomb, in an unknown country she only knows by reference or postcards, can never be like the other girls. Yes, I have always thought that I am different from what I could have been.

April was and will always be a cruel month for me, as that poet said: the month that an assassin's hand placed the Samsonite suitcase at the door of the entrance to one of the apartments occupied by the Cuban embassy in Lisbon. That bomb killed my mother and Efrén Monteagudo and could also have taken the life of my father and my two brothers who usually arrived from school at that time. I think that if I did not lose them also, it was pure coincidence, by pure chance that they were saved.

---

[1] From the testimony of Betina Palenzuela.

That year, 1976, I was in the José Martí boarding school in Artemisa. I was in seventh grade and had recently arrived from Spain where my parents were diplomats. We lived in a state of constant terror by threats and attacks, but at least we were all together. When, a year later, after concluding their mission in Spain, my father was again assigned a diplomatic post in Portugal, I had to stay in Cuba to begin my secondary school studies. My brothers Jorge and Carlos went with my parents to Lisbon and I stayed here in boarding school under the care of my grandparents with whom I spent the weekends. This period of separation was very hard. Adapt to the boarding school; make new friends, to know that I only had myself for the complexities of an adolescence I was entering. There were, of course, the letters, the telephone calls, and the satisfaction of knowing that although my parents were far away they were on a little piece of Cuba in our embassy, as it had been in Spain.

I'll never forget that day in January of 1976 when I was called because I had a visitor. It was a Friday night. I went down the stairs a bit wary. Who could come to visit me? I crossed the long corridor that separates the dormitories from the class rooms and at the end I saw the silhouette of my grandparents. Then, behind a column, I saw my mother with her kind smile and pastel blue blouse. En route through Havana, the first thing she had wanted to do was to see me, even when her sense of discipline left me there that night, until the following day when I had a pass to leave. I still could not know that it was the last time I would see her. But that image is engraved in my mind as one of my most lasting memories.

Three months later I received another visit at school. It was a Thursday, about three or four in the afternoon. It had rained and that is why we were back early from the countryside. I don't remember why I cried so much that day. During those years I cried a lot, the same as I do now when I remember those moments that keep repeating themselves in my memory, torturing me as if I were living through them all again, as if a terror film were passing through my mind and from which I could not escape.

A teacher told me that some comrades had come to get me, to gather my things that I was leaving. One of the persons waiting for me was a friend of my mother's. She only took hold of my arm strongly and put me in the car. I didn't ask anything. I knew something serious was happening but it was as if my subconscious refused to receive bad tidings. I thought it was my grandmother. We were all quiet in the car. Just before reaching my grandparent's home they told me there was an attack in the embassy in Portugal and that my mother had died there. I was speechless. I only managed to ask after my brothers of ten and eleven years of age. They told me they were all right. I could not digest the possibility that my mother was not alive. I simply did not believe it. Not even when, on the following day, I saw the news and the photographs in the newspaper and spoke with my father on the telephone. And why are you alive? I asked him. The truth was too terrible for me. Only he, my father, could give me the answer I did not want to hear. I had to hear from his lips the fearful truth: I would never again see the person who had given me my life and the one I needed most in the world.

That day, when I arrived from school, my grandparent's house was full of people. Friends, neighbors, chairs everywhere. My mother always got along well with the neighbors. She was much loved in the barrio for her simplicity and nobility. She never forgot to bring a small token from her trips for each of the persons around us. The barrio was indignant over the monstrosity of that assassination. After the details became known, all the people admired and loved her more because they learned that she lost her life through that human gesture: warning of the danger, alerting her fellow workers in the embassy, one by one, of what she had seen in the hallway, that suitcase with a bomb that killed her.

On Sunday morning the bodies of my mother and Efrén Monteagudo arrived. The funeral had to be quick as they feared the floor would give because there were so many people. I felt myself the center of all the looks. I preferred to go home with my brothers. I did not attend the funeral. For many years I lived with the fantasy that my mother was still in Portugal. I refused to admit her death.

I think the happiest years of my life are the ones I spent in Spain when we were a complete and close family, without traumas, or unbearable pains. That is why, on December 2001, when I had the opportunity of going to that country I walked twenty blocks under the snow to visit the place where I had had a family twenty six years ago.

There is something, however, that makes me proud. The day my mother died a Portuguese baby was born, the daughter of a union leader called Manuel Candeillas who was named Adriana. In her memory, because

Adriana was the name of my mother. My brother visited that girl in Portugal on the anniversary of the attack. This Portuguese girl visited Cuba when she was seventeen years old and later returned to participate in the World Festival of Youth and Students. She has been back, to our home. We communicate frequently by e-mail and have a close relationship. The Portuguese Adriana is like a symbol, a testimony of humanity and solidarity.

More than the person who carried out that act, what most impresses me and causes me greater pain is the barbarity of the act: that there could be persons in the world capable of killing innocents to overthrow a government. We, our brothers and me, were no longer able to share the important moments of our lives with a mother. If there were no more pain and deaths it was by her brave action. That is the only comforting thought.

I know that my case is not unique. I met a person who lost a much loved relative in the plane blown up in Barbados. That was a crime that occurred the same year my mother was killed. Her family, as mine, lives united by a great absence. Often words cannot transmit the pain one carries inside for always. I have lived more years than my mother lived and my brothers also and we still cannot get over it.

Yes, I have always thought that I am a different person than what I could have been. But, I am proud of my mother. And the virtues that could relate to her example, I keep well inside me, as if she were alive through me, looking at me from Portugal with a red carnation in her hands.

Havana, July, 2002

e n r i q u e   n ú ñ e z   r o d r í g u e z

METAMORFOSIS OF A NAME

The meaning of a name can change throughout a life.[1] The first Adriana I remember was a first grade teacher in a girls' school in my town. She, Ana María and Carolina Lasarte were those dedicated women who gave their lives to the education of the poorer people of my municipality. It was called a public school and was, in truth, the most private of all: deprived of books, deprived of notebooks, deprived of pencils, even deprived of desks.

Another dedicated woman, Adriana del Castillo, became a part of my reading when writing a television series that used episodes of the war during the time of Carlos Manuel de Céspedes and Francisco Vicente Aguilera.

Living in a house in Bayamo, a victim of tuberculosis, the governor Udaeta assigned a Cuban physician who served in the Spanish army to attend her. Recovering from a state of unconsciousness Adriana rejected the presence of the physician claiming that: "with that uniform you cannot cure me and I do not permit your attention"; and then she fell into unconsciousness again.

---

[1] In homage of Enrique Nuñez Rodríguez, this publication includes the text he wrote specially for the book and that is, also one of his last pieces (N. of the E.)

A few hours later Adriana opened he eyes. There was the Cuban physician who was in the Spanish army. Adriana rose from the bed in pain and began to sing: *Al combate corred bayameses, que la Patria os contempla orgullosa, no temáis una muerte gloriosa, que morir por la Patria es vivir*,[2] and collapsed definitely.

Céspedes, Fornaris and del Castillo dedicated the famous "Bayamesa" to this outstanding daughter of Luz Vázquez. Adriana gave her life in one of the most emotional moments of the history of the homeland.

Another Adriana was going to earn her place in history and was simply known as Adriana, the colleague of my daughter who worked in the Cuban Embassy in Spain. I only knew her then as the friend who cheered us up often with fresh news from Madrid.

Her name again came with a calming message: of my daughter, a young woman, who was giving birth for the first time. At the time, Adriana who was the mother of three likeable boys had decided, with the approval of her husband, Palenzuela, to move into my daughter's apartment to be with her during the hard moments of her fist delivery. Later, the photograph of Adriana arrived, holding my first grandson in her arms.

When he was just five, the grandson that we began to call "el Galleguito", exclaimed: "I was born in Madrid but at the service of the Cuban embassy so I am not a Galician, I am a Cuban".

Later Adriana was the bearer of loving messages when she came to Cuba on holiday and, some time later, together with other family news we learned that Adriana was being transferred to the embassy in Portugal. There her fate would place her in a page of history.

I will simply tell of the events as they reached me then. I have not wanted to do a historical research. I limit myself to tell them as I learned them in the most endearing family issues of that time.

These were hard days when the terrorists of Cuban origin attacked our representations abroad. One day we learned that a bomb had been placed in the building of the embassy in Portugal. The order was given to all the staff and officials to move to a room that was more protected against the expansive force of the artifact. Everyone complied with the order. Adriana

---

[2] The first stanza of the national anthem

was one of them. Then she noted the absence of the encoder who worked in one of the most vulnerable places. Without telling anyone, Adriana went to warn her colleague, Efrén Monteagudo, and that is when the bomb exploded.

Since then, for us and for all of Cuba, Adriana was not only the colleague of my daughter, an official of the Cuban embassy in Spain, the wife of Palenzuela, she became, forever, a name that will follow us all our lives: Adriana Corcho, martyr.

On April 22, 1976, a bomb placed by terrorists exploded in the Cuban Embassy in Portugal.

LADRON
DE
ALMAS

montesu0m

FLIGHT NUMBER 455 Two days later, still deeply affected by the tragedy, Rotman, flight officer in the control tower of Seawell airport in Barbados declared to the press: "But who could hate these young people? Almost all the passengers on board were young. No, no sir, not only the athletes, I said almost all. The athletes, crew, Guyanese. Eight Guyanese were students and the three others were a grandmother, daughter and grand-daughter. The girl was only nine years old. Yes sir, they were very young people. The crew also. All innocents and healthy. And if something like this could happen, precisely to them…Who can be in peace in this world?

He shook the ashes from his pipe that fell in a cone in the ashtray and then returned to his seat. On the table there was a sandwich and juice that he asked for his lunch. He decided to eat them after getting off flight number 455.

– Seawell ramp, CU–455 prepared for take off.

Rotman hears the Cubana pilot's voice, takes the mike in his hand and presses the carrier

– CU–455 received, authorized for take off. Temperature 30, altimeter pressure 29,94.

– CU–455 received.

He watched the plane through the tower windows. Waited for authorization for the next maneuver. A few minutes later he heard

– CU–455 authorized for revving

– CU–455 authorized for thrust.

– Received

He watched the plane turn and then communicated:

– CU–455 authorized to taxi right front, along taxiway-Alpha waiting point, use second intersection, time 11.

The metal giant began to move slowly to the end of the runway, turned 180 degrees and stopped.

– CU–455 authorized for Norman Manley, red route 11, we maintain a 350 degree right turn.

Rotman presses again the carrier mike button.

– CU-455 authorized for take-off, surface winds 09508.

Wilfredo accelerated and then giving power to the four motors for take-off began to taxi on the runway. He increased speed and lifted off after speeding up for two thousand three hundred meters.

It was twelve fifteen. Rotman prepared to contact CU-455 for the last time.

– CU–455 take off 15, change to over 119,7. Report arrival of flight 180. Good day.

After the pilot of flight 455 of Cubana de Aviación airline confirmed to the tower that it would inform when the plane reaches the height of eighteen thousand feet. Rotman leans back in his seat and took a bite of his sandwich.

The rejoicing in the plane continued spontaneously. After the tragedy, witnesses in Barbados said that the athletes boarding the flight were enjoying themselves. That is why no one noted the two seats up front that were empty. The Venezuelans, Hernán Ricardo, who had shown a false passport and Freddy Lugo had occupied them on the short trip (twenty-six minutes) from Trinidad to Barbados. On disembarking they had completed the mission of placing bombs in a Cubana flight making its regular flight from Guyana to Havana, with a stop-over in Trinidad and Tobago, Barbados, Jamaica and Santiago de Cuba. They had been preparing the mission for several months under directions of Hernán, Luis Posada Carriles and another well known anti-Castro figure, Orlando Bosch Avila, considered by the FBI as the number 1 terrorist in America. Everything was ready, every detail adjusted with the precision of a watchmaker. That is why, in spite of the setbacks and obstacles they had to avoid that day, Hernán and Lugo, on disembarking in Barbados and losing themselves in the city crowd, knew that the plane would not reach its destination.

Everything began at dawn when the flight captain prepared to take off from Timehri in Guyana. The control tower reported that the government requested a delay for a delegation traveling to Havana in route to their country. Wilfredo could not refuse. The request had come from high up. The interruption meant a twenty-seven minute delay.

For this reason, when Hernán Ricardo and Freddy Lugo arrived at Piarco airport in Trinidad and Tobago, the second stop-over, asked about the Cubana flight they were told it was delayed. In statements to the Police after the arrest of the terrorists, Charles Murray, traffic assistant offered to put them on a flight of Sunjet Service of BWIA that had a stop-over in Barbados in route to Miami. Very upset, Hernán kept moving his head from side to side. Mr. Murray, according to his statements included in the bulky court file, thought that perhaps they had not understood since he spoke to them in English. Then he pointed to the BWIA add and said in Spanish: "Barbados now". Ricardo exclaimed "No!" Although the answer was categorical, Murray, not understanding the reasons for this insistence called a member of the Cuban sports group over to the desk (they had arrived the morning before on a flight from Venezuela) asking him to serve as interpreter as he had talked to him in English earlier. The unexpected incident, completely unplanned and that compromised the terrorists should have been enough to abort the plan. But Hernán, completely unperturbed, smiled to the young man standing in front of him and insisted on his wish to board the Cubana flight that was promptly translated to Murray who thanked him and issued the tickets. A short while later the two terrorists learned that the employees who had offered their services were on strike. Another unexpected situation.

The Cuban plane arrived in Trinidad and Tobago at eleven in the morning, local time. By radio, the captain was informed of the impossibility of using

119

the cleaning and refueling services due to the strike. Wilfredo decided to take the services in Barbados.

Anxious to arrive as soon as posible to the large island, he requested permission from the airport authorities to allow the passengers to carry the equipment themselves onto the storage compartment. Four athletes enjoying the adventure of driving the luggage cars and carrying it on board completed the operation in record time. Also the contagious enthusiasm spread to all the passengers: to arrive home as soon as possible without losing another minute.

Belkys and Daniel walked slowly hand in hand. She looked at the passengers who were preparing to board the Cubana flight. She read the emotion in the eyes of that girl over her adventure accompanied by her favorite doll. Those young people who hugged the mother, the father, the brothers and were locked in a fiery kiss to the girlfriend. "Study hard". "Write when you arrive". "Don't fail to go to mass". Belkys thought they were students who had won a scholarship to study in the Island. She was not mistaken.

– Are you part of the crew of Cubana de Aviación? – Belkys and Daniel slowed down – At what time do we arrive in Havana? – the woman asked.

– If we leave on time and have no more delays – Daniel looked at his watch – at five thirty more or less.

– My husband is a fishery official and has just completed his contract. We are returning definitely to Cuba; ten years away has been too much.

– The Canary Islands, Mexico and now the Caribbean – the man said without any sign of pride – But this was the last mission – he concluded.

– And the last plane – the woman added.

Daniel and Belkys stepped back. On the steps to the plane they stopped.

– I'll be back in a week – he said and they kissed strongly, as is common among sweethearts. They had been married several weeks ago and this flight would take them home to continue their interrupted honeymoon for reasons of work. But at the last minute he was asked to stay on in Trinidad and Tobago for a switch with another crew member who was scheduled to fly over the Atlantic and had taken sick suddenly. Daniel was a flight engineer and Belkys a stewardess.

120

– I love you – he said pushing her away softly.

– It's the first time we fly apart, I'm going to miss you – she added and they kissed again.

While Bebo, the flight attendant, counted the food trays, Teresa sprayed air freshener in the bathrooms and re–supplied them. She checked emergency supplies: bottles of oxygen, extinguishers, and life saver vests – placed under the seats.

For several months she checked for any object that did not correspond to airplane equipment. Then all the crew of this route were called to a meeting and for four hours a Cuban Security official instructed them on a series of measures to be taken before and during the trip to prevent possible terrorist actions.

– Are you going to Cuba? – Belkys asked the Indian looking girl.

– No – she smiled back – I'm going to Jamaica.

– You have very beautiful hair – Belkys told her while she adjusted her safety belt.

– So do my dolls.

Belkys smiled and noted two women, also dark skinned, who accompanied the girl. "Mother and grandmother" – she commented. The older of the two denied with a shake of the head –: aunt, she corrected, and placed a nylon bag on the rug in front of the girl's feet.

– It seems that these young people are going to Cuba to study – Belkys said and looked at the passengers sitting across.

– It's true – said one in perfect Spanish –. How did you know?

– Ah, stewardesses develop an acute sense of observation. Thanks to that I noted that you intended to light a cigarette and I will have to tell you not to while the sign is still on.

The Guyanese promptly put the cigarette back in the pack while they continued to watch through their tinted lenses. The three had eyeglasses with corrections. It was obvious that they felt like newborns if their whole life was centered on being on this plane where their real life was going to begin.

Sitting in the last seats were the fishery official and his wife. Both were happy to be going home. Belkys greeted them and checked their safety belts.

– Look.

Belkys took the photograph the woman was showing her. It was the photo of a baby with only his face showing above the sheets as if getting out from hiding with a broad mischievous smile.

– He is very pretty – Belkys said and discovered a spark of pride in the couple.

Minutes later the plane was in flight.

A short distance from the pilot's cabin, Octavio and Kiko, fencing trainers, occupied the first passenger seats.

– Did she go to bed with you?

– She didn't want to.

– Ah! So then you asked her and she turned you down.

Octavio's expression didn't fool Kiko.

– Are you making fun of me?

– Meeeee!! – Octavio put his hand on his chest.

—¡Yoooouu!

– Go to hell.

– Kiko got up and went to the back of the plane, upset.

Octavio was satisfied. Now he could stretch out on the seats.

He noticed the little girl opposite. She is really very pretty.

Octavio remembered his little girl and Leila, his wife. He closed his eyes and imagined them at the airport.

A bit further back one of the Guyanese students made efforts to communicate with Alex, the new Central American fencing champion.

– Cuba…medicine…doctor.

– You're going to study medicine, that's good. But doctor, no way, it's still far off. You have the lock but are lacking the key.

– Lock, what?

– Forget it bro and have a drink.

Alex took out a bottle from his jacket pocket with a disapproving look from Magaly.

– Don't go getting drunk – she interrupted the conversation.

The Guyanese took a drink and licked his lip.

– Are you a student?

122

– Yeah, student, yeah, fencer.

– What's that?

Alex sketched a feint in the air.

– Painter?

– Hell…what's this?

Alex took off his safety belt and lowered his hand luggage that had a sword sticking out. He showed it to him and from his pocket he took out his medal.

– Oooooh! I see, you're a sportsman.

The Guyanese took another drink and returned the bottle to Alex who copied him. Later he sat back in the cushioned seat grinning widely. Next to him, Magaly looked at him from the corner of her eye and pocked him with her elbow.

—— Let's see if you arrive in Havana drunk and your father has to carry you to the Matrimony Palace.

Magaly and Alex were fiancées and where getting married that evening. The families of both had made all the preparations.

Hernán and Lugo were seated behind the Guyanese family. They left the center seat unoccupied and placed their hand luggage there. Hernán took out a flask out of his and took a drink of rum. When he withdrew the small glass cap from his lips he saw the head of the little Guyanese girl slowly raising her head up the back of the seat. Then the bright black eyes appeared.

Felicita and Robertico, the youngest athletes, were sitting together and both tried to break the silence that was becoming embarrassing. Ever since they left Havana, this was the first time they were alone, as much alone as you can on a plane. But they also knew that they were there right next to each other through the complicity of both. Their looks gave them away.

Felicita felt that something was happening on board. She felt that her life was going to go through a radical change and that in the future, being alone could only be considered if her thoughts were on him.

Everything would begin in that plane, during the flight back home and that would end going down the stairs, holding hands. But knowing him well, she knew it would not be an easy task, but a challenge instead, and began to feel uneasy.

And again she bit her nails.

She had made up her mind although she would have to court him. That is why she was surprised when Robertico, after helping her adjust her safety belt, gave her the tape recorder and said: "The tape is at the beginning, listen to it".

And now, with her earphones on, her face began to light up while her heart started to beat rapidly and the emotion caught in her throat.

In one of the last seats, Irene was reading a book on architecture. She had just started her third year and would have to take several tests that had added up during the competition.

Next to her Gallo held on tightly to the seat arms. He was suddenly startled.

– It's only a tape recorder – she said to calm him –. Planes are safer than cars. Much safer – she stressed.

In the aisle, Rosa the foil fencer of the young team, started to swing her hips to the rhythm of the Bonny M to the beating palms of Alex, who had gone back with his Guyanese friend.

– Ham and cheese sandwiches, juices and peanuts – Teresa said while she checked the tray. She popped some peanuts into her mouth and took the tray in her hands.

In her fifteen years of service she had flied almost all the routes of Cubana de Aviación but she had never felt so tired as this one of Havana–Guyana: three stopovers, two of only thirty minutes, passengers in, passengers off, farewells, welcomes, smiles down, smiles up, instructions, candies, breakfast, beverages, drinks, coffee, packs, aspirins. When she thought that she could finally catch a few minutes, a light in the *galley* lit up: landing. And start all over again.

But even so, she preferred to fly this route. For two years, no problems. Not like those crossing the Atlantic, in those old planes that even the most enlightened called *La milagrosa* (The miraculous). The fire that began in the galley and spreading rapidly, trying to devour it all. Or the descent in Madrid without landing gear. Or that passenger, Czech or Bulgarian – she never found out – who died in her arms: she wrapped him with a blanket and only told the curious "He has a fever". And the sea landing. The minutes of anxiety that followed the announcement by the captain: "Ladies and gentlemen, for technical difficulties – oil that was slipping out

124

threatened to disintegrate the plane – we will proceed to a sea landing. Please remove your shoes and pay attention to the instructions of the crew. Thank you very much." Before she didn't know if she would be able enjoy her old age with her grandson that was expected. Now, on the other hand …

– Do we tell the passengers to disembark in Seawell? – Teresa asked the captain in the cabin and looked out on the sea in front of the nose of the DC–8.

– No, no – Wilfredo doubted, but changed his mind instantly – : We have to load up the services we couldn't in Piarco; yes have them disembark. The trip to Jamaica is long.

Hernán checked what he would do in five minutes: he would open the bag, take out the camera pack with the bomb inside, he'd put it in a pants pocket and would go to the bathroom. Later the announcement of arrival in Barbados would be announced. That is why he shuddered when he heard the voice of the airline stewardess announcing the arrival in a few minutes.

First he looked at Lugo – sitting on the outer seat – who made a strange grimace. And later, the bag. Then he opened it, took out the photo camera and put it in his pocket.

He went out into the aisle and walked up.

He passed by Alex who was about to take a drink from his bottle. He overheard when the young man seated next to the youth, in what seemed like a Caribbean accent:

– Hey kid, this is like pumpkin for me, it is neither good for me or bad, quite the contrary.

– You're going to drive him crazy – he heard the young woman sitting next to him say.

Felicita and Robertico did not notice him. She had her eyes closed and he was whispering in her ear holding his hand in hers.

He walked ahead and stopped in front of Rosa who was blocking the aisle trying to move aside. On the seat a tape recorder was playing *reggae* music.

– Didn't you hear the stewardess? – He placed his hands on the back of the seats and rolled his eyes and growled – She's not at home.

Rosa went back, took the tape recorder in her hands and sat down. She clucked her tongue but the eyes looking at the terrorist were radiant. She knew that there were only three hours that separated from her family that Alex called "the many". Surely her father had rented a bus for all the family and was on the way to the airport. A longshoreman at the docks, he was proud of the youngest one of the numerous offspring who had received most affection because she was conceived at an age that children and grand-children are together.

– Please

Belkys was right behind Hernán who moved to let her pass.

– You must go back to your seat. We are getting ready to land.

The fishery official and his wife looked out at the coast.

In the back seat, Irene did the same. She was thinking that at this time her father would be at the dairy farm after the second milking, adding honeys to the fodder, filling the water trough or curing ailment. All the memories of her father linked him to that routine. She only saw him with a *guayabera* once and it was very tight: the day that he went to the train station to see her off after allowing her to accept the sports scholarship in the capital. Irene watched the beaches below.

The small island of Barbados, only four hundred thirty square kilometers and two hundred fifty thousand inhabitants, could be seen below surrounded by a sea, like an oasis. The barbuda fig forests, from which island derives its name, covered the coast right up to the sand of the beach.

A few seconds later, Hernán shut himself in toilet number two. He pressed the lock and washed his face with his free hand. While he listened to the sizzling of the urine he thought of the faces the passengers would put at the moment of the explosion, terrified, torn to bits, burned. He took out the camera case and placed it on the washbasin. He finished urinating. Then he took the bomb again and sat on the floor in front of the washbasin. He noted that there was a compartment with an opening to receive discarded napkins.

He placed a leg against the partition and pulled the compartment that gave way. They he took the camera case and opened it. The explosive was in view and in the center the upper part of the fuse.

He dried the sweat speckling his forehead, looked at the time and pressed the copper with his thumb and forefinger until he felt the acid bulb break.

The tightened copper wire began to be eaten up. Seconds later he withdrew the security pin, leaving the way free for the hammer. He knew that in forty five minutes, when the wire holding it broke, it would project into the percussion cap making the explosion.

He closed the case again.

Very carefully, like a first time father, he placed the bomb in the compartment, closed the partition and pushed it in softly.

Posada and Bosch had told him that the cleaning services on board were done in Trinidad and Tobago and that is why the stopover in Barbados would be only fifteen or twenty minutes.

In his seat, in the front part of the plane, Lugo seemed to be tuning the radio he had in his hand. In truth, he had just crushed the bulb that was hidden inside.

Another bomb.

Hernán urinated again and then tried to get out. Then it happened. The door didn't open. He pressed again and nothing. He checked the safety and noticed that he had pushed it back. He was locked inside, less than a meter from the bomb mechanism that had begun its countdown.

He paled visibly and his fingers grabbed the lock. His eyelids turned red while he pulled on the door.

– Miss! Miss!

His words came out strong although he tried to contain the panic.

– Miss, get me out of here! – he dried the sweat from his face.

– What's the matter, sir?

It was the voice of Belkys who tried uselessly to open the door.

– Who is it?

– I'm stuck – he shouted, banging on the door repeatedly.

Shortly alter a deep voice was heard.

– Take off the safety latch! – Bebo said with determination. Hernán obeyed.

A few seconds later, the door opened. Hernán's face was livid, his shirt wet with perspiration and he was breathing with difficulty. Bebo watched him. Belkys looked into his face. Teresa noted something.

– These Russian planes are shit.

He almost spit out the last word.

– The only thing that happened to you is that you didn't release the safety latch – Bebo said and leaned over to demonstrate –. Also, this plane is from the US.

– Return to your seat we are about to land – Belkys told him.

In his outer seat, Lugo had turned and was looking out the window.

Belkys placed one of the seats of the one of the Guyanese students in an upright position. She wondered if she should tell the captain about her concern over the strange conduct of the passenger that had crossed her mind before. She remembered that Teresa had told her that the destination of the passenger was Barbados and the island was already in view.

A few seats back Hernán covered his face appearing to be reading a newspaper to avoid the curious looks of the passenger but he couldn't understand the words. His nerves were shot and he was extremely anxious wanting to get up from his seat and run to the door. But his fright wasn't because of the acid that was burning the tension wire of the bomb, nor because of the close to hundred passengers around him whose lives meant less to him than a flock on their way to the slaughterhouse but because of that damn door that didn't give way. Yes, he had a sign from the Lord. What he didn't understand was the delay. Why when he had activated it?

A few minutes later, while he disembarked he felt eyes on his back. Several times this morning he had the same feeling on his neck.

The plane shook at twelve twenty three, local time.

In the control cabin, a few seconds before, Wilfredo had given over command to the copilot and was preparing to inform Seawell the reaching of eighteen thousand feet. At the very moment that he pushed the talk button on the microphone he felt that the plane was being torn apart.

– Be careful! – he shouted.

He took control of the ship and rapidly looked at the panel. He discovered yellow lights in one of the discs. That moment the siren under the flight engineer went off. Then he had no doubt: the pressure had gone down suddenly.

A dry blow behind him indicated that the cabin door had been opened with violence and began to feel vibrations that are produced when the fuselage has been damaged. He held on tightly to the flight rudder.

Next to him, the copilot also heard the blow of the door when it opened suddenly and turned his body to look along the aisle to the passenger cabin. He saw enough to make his blood freeze. Then he had no doubt: and expansive wave of a powerful explosion had violently ripped off the door lock.

– Shut the door! – he yelled and prepared to isolate the cabin from the black smoke and those screams that were beginning to invade the plane –. Something exploded in the back and there is fire – he said with emotion.

– Inform Seawell – Wilfredo ordered and his voice sounded sure. He was trying to level off the plane, he pushed the rudder in slowly and the plane dipped its nose. Then he took the brake and pulled it in.

Above, the wing flaps lifted and the speed began to slow down.

In the control tower, the workers were busy with their routine.

Two planes had landed and another was in the air, still within the radial perimeter of the airport. Rotman was eating his sandwich absent-mindedly while he looked at his left with attention, where the radio equipment was. He thought he heard something unusual because of its brevity, a word he didn't understand and a wave of static that sounded when the carrier button was pressed in the microphone.

He noted that the equipment operator was inclined forward and his face was shadowed with vexation. Then he realized that he was not mistaken. Something had happened in one of the two planes he had in flight. At that moment he heard a terrified but strong and sure voice.

– Seawell! Seawell! — CU-455!

Rotman frowned while he opened the talk key:

– CU–455 … Seawell.

– We have an explosion on board and are descending rapidly! There is fire on board!

Rotman spit out the pieces of bread, ham and cheese and pushed his seat and took the microphone from the young operator. He cleared his throat and pressed the carrier.

– CU–455 are you coming back?

He had no response from the plane.

Half a dozen men working in the control tower surrounded the radio and stared at the speaker, anxious to hear the Cuban.

Rotman didn't repeat the question. He knew that the captain would check the damages before responding. If the answer was affirmative it would be a sign that something serious was happening in the Cubana 455 that had taken off eight minutes ago. Something that could not be controlled by the crew.

While he waited, he turned the radar screen and located the plane.

– It's at twenty eight miles – the operator said after making the calculations.

At that moment Rotman noticed how the plane was beginning a right turn. He waited no longer.

He turned and located the red button on the wall above the control panel and pressed it. It was the emergency sign.

The explosion on board the plane was a devastating flash, horrifying.

The moment of the explosion, Belkys was welcoming the passengers over the speakers. Her voice was quickly interrupted, like howl of a drowning kitten and everything in the plane flew into the air.

In the fuselage the explosion tore out an opening of about a meter in diameter. The air in the plane lost pressure and there was an escape of contained air. Uncontrollable, the force of suction dragged everything in its way: bags, trays, refreshment bottles, tins of juice and beer, glasses, candy that was being offered, arms, legs, viscera …

Automatically the compartments above the seats opened freeing the oxygen masks linked by plastic tubes to a central deposit.

Suddenly the suction diminished but the fire in the front was spreading together with something more deadly: the smoke.

The bomb had exploded under seat number twenty six where the little Guyanese girl sat. The burst tore her right leg off and the expansive wave was so strong that the security belt cut into her stomach until being tuck the hip bones. Her long black straight hair that must have been the pride of her parents was now a burnt tangled mass of black wire. For several seconds after the explosion, he eyes flickered with intensity, amazement and, finally, fear. Then the little girl died. The aunt and grandmother were a mass of flesh and bones.

Teresa was walking in the aisle and the force of the explosion threw her against the roof, she rebounded and fell back, dying.

Panic had invaded the passengers. Some stayed tied by their safety belts, with oxygen masks on, moving their eyes from side to side, trying to understand what happened. Other ran in desperation looking for a place to escape from the smoke.

Those who had managed to flee from the center of the plane where the explosion occurred gathered at the back.

– Calm down! Calm down! – Belkys and Bebo tried to make themselves heard.

– Be quiet, damn it! – Bebo began to pull open the doors of the tour toilet. When he managed to open one he called to the passengers who were writhing, spitting, coughing, vomiting black smoke – Inside, drink water and wet your faces!

With one look at their faces he understood that they were terrified and paralyzed by fear. Suddenly the black cloud began to dissipate. Bebo realized that the captain had opened the windows at the back of the plane and the smoke now blew out.

The smoke cleared enough and then he saw her. In the aisle, on the rug, there was a woman with her leg shattered. The bone had broken through and splintered and the bloody flesh could be seen. What impressed him most was that the woman barely complained, she just looked at what was left of her leg. Next to her another wounded passenger called for a doctor.

Those first moments almost everyone was out of their minds with fear. Only a few overcame their terror, they advised, begged, demand, trying uselessly to control those who were hysterical.

Bebo looked down the aisle and saw the fire. He took the extinguisher and ran to them. If he could not put out the fire, it would spread. Then the opened windows would not be enough and the smoke would spread along that steel tube where they were now stuck.

– Get away! He screamed and then emptied the extinguisher into the flames and threw it down; he turned and ran down the aisle vomiting smoke. He crossed the toilet, separated Rosa who was wetting her face and pressed the water faucet. With his free hand he threw water on his hot face.

The toasted flesh of Alex burned and he howled like a bull. He opened his eyes and saw a great red flash. He tried to get up, overcoming the pain; the burns reached his soul. Magaly had stropped screaming and her body began to burn. Alex writhed at her side. A terrified scream escaped from his throat. His body was a human torch.

A few meters back, Octavio noticed the empty extinguisher that was swaying on the rug. He heard the screams of terror from the front and thought he heard the deep voice of Alex.

His mind shuddered. He turned and found the frozen eyes of a dead passenger. He mouth was very open. He rapidly turned back and hit his head on the window and closed his eyes. Some metal shards had hit his back, damaging his spine and now he could not move his body.

Behind, a Guyanese student tried to move the motionless body of one of his compatriots. He had released the safety belt and was going to carry him when he saw a huge gap in his chest. Moving him, the boy fell to the floor and began to shake violently. His leg kept kicking against the rug uncontrollably, while the other Guyanese tried to lift him. Unable to carry him he dragged him to the back section of the plane. Bebo came across them.

– Put the oxygen mask on him!

Later he released the extinguisher foam over the flames. When these subsided a bit he saw, horrified, a small body stained in red. To reach it he had to overcome a twisted mass. The seats were like sharp knives. He tried to jump over them but his right leg got caught and he felt the skin rip. He ignored the pain when he discovered the disfigured face of the little Guyanese girl. His stomach turned and bile rose to his throat. He coughed smoke and felt hot and suffocated. Before turning back he looked and the shattered body of the little girl who held on strongly to the doll that, miraculously, was intact and with its eyes very open.

Bebo understood that the passengers near the explosion were dead or seriously injured and nothing could be done for them. Turning back he noticed the face of the man sitting in the window seat. It was Octavio. His eyes were closed and his head rested on the window. His face was covered in blood.

Bebo continued on back. He lifted the body of Teresa and placed it on the empty seats. He decided to go to the galley to get another fire extinguisher. He felt a strong hot flash in his bladder and stopped at a toilet. He asked the passengers in the toilet to leave it for a moment and since these, two men and one woman, all squeezed in the one meter square space looked at him with indifference and he went to another one.

132

While he listened to his urine he asked himself if he would get out of this hell alive.

Since the explosion, two minutes ago, made the plane shudder, Irene held tightly onto the seat. She had put on the oxygen mask and helped Gallo. His eyes were popping and terror choked his voice.

– Talk, say something, speak – Irene insisted again but Gallo was speechless.

He put his hand on his chest and squeezed tight his eyes, resisting a strong pain.

– It hurts – he complained.

Irene put the oxygen mask on him, thinking that perhaps he couldn't breathe well.

– Take a deep breath – she begged him –. It seems we are going back to the airport.

She had noticed a slight inclination of the wings from the window.

– We are going back – she repeated to Gallo.

Belkys passed checking the oxygen masks and calming everyone down.

Irene looked at her disheartened and she leaned down to touch the face of Gallo.

– We are a few minutes from the airport – she said and coughed. She placed the portable oxygen mask to her face and took a deep breath.

Belkys went to the back of the plane.

– The worst is over, do you hear – Irene whispered to Gallo. But his face tightened with pain.

– The saint made no mistake – his voice was barely audible –. I'm going to die.

He complained again and tried to lean forward but his seat belt held him back.

Irene looked around her and discovered a dense cloud of smoke that was moving over her head. Gallo let his head fall back and his neck muscles became rigid. Irene barely heard him. A few seconds later his stony eyes stared out at her.

His shiny brown eyes opened wide and a grimace came over his face in pain. He placed his hand on his chest and leaned forward. He writhed about and would have fallen to the floor had it not been for the seat belt.

Irene had never seen death before.

She rested her head on the seat. She wanted to close her eyes and imagine it was last year, last week, the day before. Any moment before that blast.

Behind her the wife of the Fishery official had begun to pray while she held on the arm of her husband who held the mask to her.

– God! – The voice of the woman was calm – don't let these children die, they are children. *Our Father who art in Heaven hallowed be thy name...*

Sobbing and trembling, Felicita hugged the flight attendant.

– I want to see my mother – she sighed.

That moment, the telephone rang in the galley and Bebo rushed to take it. At his side Belkys coughed several times until she threw up. With one hand Bebo took the phone while he held Felicita with the other.

– Speak, hello, I can't hear you!

Belkys knelt on the rug and seemed to calm down after breathing in several times from the portable oxygen bottle. Bebo replaced his and inhaled while he saw a very young fencer a few meters back, putting away a tape recorder in his bag. It seemed ridiculous.

– Bebo, it's me, tell me what's happening back there.

– There's fire and a lot of smoke – he screamed –. There was an explosion in the center and there are many dead – he paused then –; Teresa is dead. Do you hear me? There is fire and the worse is the smoke that is suffocating us.

– Are you using the masks?

– It's difficult to keep the people in their seats. The worse is the smoke – he insisted and coughed several times.

– Keep calm – the voice of the flight engineer sounded comforting, although he imagined what was happening in the passenger section –. Buckle in. We are going back to Seawell!

Communication was cut and Bebo realized that the line had been cut some where, probably by the fire. He stopped trying to communicate again and bent down to Belkys.

He wiped the perspiration with his handkerchief. She looked up at him with eyes made teary by the smoke and tears and with a firm voice told him:

– Those who got off in Barbados – Bebo frowned without understanding –. The one who got stuck in the bathrooms... she managed to say.

134

Bebo opened his eyes wide.

– The sons of bitches – he exclaimed. His eyes were wide and his lips trembled –, the sons of bitches!

When he hung up, the flight engineer told the captain what was happening in the passenger section.

Knocking was heard on the door again.

– Don't open – Wilfredo yelled.

If they had opened the smoke would have filled the cabin.

Since the explosion, about two minutes and forty seven seconds ago, everything occurred very fast.

– Call back and report that we are returning – he ordered the copilot holding tightly onto the rudder vibrating with the wounded plane.

– OK, Seawell, CU.455, we request immediately, immediately, runway!

In the control tower they heard the emotive voice of the copilot.

Rotman answered:

– CU-455 authorized to land.

He knew that it was in answer to a question before. He understood watching the turn the plane was making on the radar screen.

He stretched his arm and communicated through the land control frequency, with the airport fire chief who had his men on alert

– Total emergency – Rotman said –, flight CU–455 with an explosion and fire on board, he will touch down on runway one – making a fast calculation he added – in about seven minutes.

– Is it very serious? – The voice of the airport fire chief sounded familiar.

– I'm afraid so, Andrew – Rotman answered and sighed –. I fear the worst.

Hanging up he gazed at the radar screen.

– Sir – the tower team operator said, without hiding the emotion he felt –, the turn of Cubana is too wide. The speed is two hundred twenty knots way below for that height. I suggest you tell the captain to make a tighter turn and increase speed.

Rotman sat back in his chair. The green light continued to shine in the radar screen. Those in the tower looked at Rotman and didn't understand his silence. He continued to watch the lit screen. The speed of the plane, close to four hundred kilometers an hour was, in truth, below what was established for that height and the turn to return to the airport was too wide.

Logically, in an emergency of this kind, a spiraling turn had to be made, descending rapidly and reaching the airport in the shortest time possible.

– No, no – Rotman said moving his head. He had broken the silence.

In the tower, those present understood that the chief wouldn't make these indications to the pilot and asked themselves why.

Rotman was calm. He wasn't concerned that in the floor below there were tape recorders that registered all the conversations between the land and air for future reference. He knew what to say to justify his denial. But the mere fact of thinking what kept the Cubana pilot from turning and coming down faster, made him shudder.

Inside the Cubana 455 command cabin, the pilots were tense. Three minutes and thirty one seconds separated them from the voice: "Take care!" and since then they seemed to have aged.

Wilfredo grasped the rudder fighting the vibrations and the trembling of the plane. These convulsions and sudden depressurization confirmed that the explosion had ripped an opening in the fuselage seriously damaging the structure in some point with the following danger that the opening would increase. For this reason he was forced to make a pronounced turn and descend to a lesser speed than what was indicated in these cases. If he forced the ship it would disintegrate in the air.

– Lower the landing gear! Flaps in point zero!

The copilot obeyed. He understood what the chief was trying; the pressure of the air on the wheels would increase the descent. This maneuver is known by pilots as dirtying the plane.

He fought to descend rapidly for another reason: he knew the oxygen released automatically fed the flames. The oxygen valves were opened automatically when the plan altitude reached between ten thousand five hundred fourteen feet and closed again when it was at eight thousand feet. That is why he always checked the altimeter that now marked twelve thousand. He still had to descend four thousand feet more for the valves to stop feeding the fire ball he feared had filled the passenger cabin, by the terrifying screams behind the door.

Bebo discharged the contents of another extinguisher on the bodies of several passengers. When the fires receded, he was paralyzed: covered in

136

foam, totally carbonized were the two bodies of Alex and Magaly intertwined and twisted.

On the seat, close to the couple, he discovered another body, also burned. The arms gripped the seat in a position that Bebo thought impossible.

The flames came back and he began to cough exhaling the black smoke that threatened to cover him. He withdrew.

Reaching the galley he had another coughing attack. Belkys who had recovered for a few moments offered the portable tank and Bebo filled his lungs with oxygen.

– Mother! – she said in a soft voice –. Is there no way to put this fire out and get the smoke out?

Around her, on the floors and in the narrow toilets, the survivors were gathered, coughing, vomiting, crying, and shouting.

The heat in that part of the plane was about sixty degrees.

Bebo returned the mask to Belkys who was on the verge of fainting.

– We should be over the runway – he told her and Belkys did not seem to listen. The scarce forces she had threatened to abandon her and the flight attendant held her for the second time to prevent her from falling. He helped her to sit on the rug. He looked around and his eyes stopped at Rosa and Felicita. Both seemed very young, almost children. They were seated, embracing in the interior of one of the toilets and, with their faces close together, were breathing from the same oxygen tank.

Bebo tried to stand up but his legs wouldn't hold him. He let himself fall and dragged himself out of the toilet. He rested his back on the emergency door. He began to lose consciousness of reality and was aware of it. Everything was in chaos.

He felt an enormous weight on his wounded leg. He had never gone through something like this and perhaps would not see the end.

– Shit! – He exclaimed and saw Belkys fall beside him, on the rug covered by a thick layer of soot.

For the first time, the truth of what had happened hit him like a slap in the face.

In one of the back rows of seats, Robertico gripped the mask. He pressed it and inhaled desperately but felt that the air did not enter his lungs. The last rain of the seventeen pounds of oxygen of his tank had just been expelled. He could get another but he did not have the strength.

The next mask was almost in his reach.

He felt his heart beating in his chest and a strong pressure exploding in his head. He was inhaling the black lethal smoke. A strong breath passed from his lungs to his brains.

To run, flee, escape anywhere was his only alternative. Barely managing, he released his safety belt, rode and ran looking for the exit. When he found it he began to bang it with legs and hands and finally with his head while he screamed in terror:

– Get me out of here! Get me out of here!

At his feet, Bebo tried uselessly to take the almost empty portable oxygen tank.

Robertico fell beside him, without strength and dizzy. He let himself fall on the hot and black rug and covered his face with his hands that shook violently.

– I don't want to die – he sobbed.

The smoke continued to fill his lungs and now invaded his brain.

He coughed repeatedly until he began to retch, deep death rattle like the banging of bones inside his chest. His mouth was open and he tried to scream but could not get any sound out. Then his vision fogged up. He began to move his arms around and shake his legs with violence.

A fish on the boat deck.

By that time four minutes and fifty seven seconds had passed after the explosion that had caused the death by suffocation or burning of more than fifty passengers.

Suddenly, the release of oxygen was cut and the masks hung limply. In truth very few were able to use them. The soot covered the upper part of doors, screens, seats and, in spite of the opened windows; it was not enough to decontaminate the air. The wood, cotton, paper and plastic, all materials used in the interior passenger cabin furniture and other pillows, grills, wool of the seats, when they began to decompose by the heat, let off toxic gasses: carbon monoxide, hydrogen cyanide, fluoride acid, chloride acid and nitrogen dioxide.

The inhalation of these toxic gasses, combined, is more lethal than when breathed separately.

Now, crammed in this steel sarcophagus, the few surviving passengers fought desperately to fill their lungs with the little pure air that entered the plane by the opening and the low altitude vents.

138

Through the window, Octavio observed down below that was coming closer. For a few seconds he contemplated the space in all its immensity. Lines of all shades of blue. A seagull glided softly on its calm and slow flight. The heat was now intense. The trainer heard the crack of wood and saw the plastic melt.

He screamed, but it was lost amidst others farther away. He thought that everyone on the plane had gone crazy. He rested his head against the window and looked up to the sky. The sun was there. In his mind, the image of Leila appeared. He saw her preparing the boy to go to the airport. His eyes clouded up.

Octavio was right. At that time his wife was on the point of leaving for the airport. Before he made sure that Tavito's bladder was empty and checked to see if the pudding was cool. Then she put it in the refrigerator. It was Octavio's favorite desert. An hour later she reached the airport.

– The flight is delayed – the employee answered and left the counter. He knew that the plane had had an accident but he was following orders of the manager. On the terrace, she noted an unaccustomed turmoil on the runways that, at first, she thought it was a plane being brought out from the hangar. When it was parked she discovered that it had the logo of the Cuban Red Cross. Then she went down and repeated her question to the employee.

– At what time does Cubana from Guyana arrive?

The answer stopped her short. The man had told her that the flight was delayed due to technical problems and advised her to go home and keep in telephone contact.

Leaving the airport with Tavito asleep over her shoulder, four Cuban sports officials got out of a car. None approached her although they knew her (Leila had been a member of the national fencing team). They only gave a cold wave at a distance and hurried on. During her return home she asked the taxi driver to tune into the radio but heard no disturbing news. When she arrived home she called her brother-in-law. He left for the airport while she put her three year old boy to sleep and sat in the sidewalk to wait. By midnight Octavio's brother got out of a car, embraced her and holding back his sobs said:

– They're all dead.

Two weeks later they discovered the pudding still in the refrigerator. It hadn't been touched.

The night of October 6 was a fateful day for the relatives of the travelers of flight 455. In the future nothing in their lives would be the same.

"The many" left the airport the following morning only after the manager assured them for the third time, that there were no survivors. They would never get together again. Rosa's father retired shortly after. Then he dedicated his time to match the women's fencing tournaments, silent and distant, although he had never understood the complexities of fencing.

When, on the following morning, Irene's husband got out of a jeep at the entrance of the faro, the old campesino did not come out onto the road as he was accustomed to do. He heard the news apparently impassible while he wrung his hat in his hands. He turned and disappeared in the nearby forest. He returned only the following morning, wet by the dew, his head down and his eyes bloodshot. In the patio in the house, a pig on a spit was half baked that was being devoured by vultures.

Sunday morning he used to sit in the porch of the bohio leaning back on the stool, against the wall, looking over the newspaper photos of his daughter Irene, alive.

Months later, the Canadian insurance company, owners of the plane, deposited a large sum of money in the hands of the campesino. He returned it to the puzzled lawyer who, in face of the hard look of that man, gave up any idea of insisting.

In Alex's house the preparations for his marriage were intact. Left on the table were the cake, snacks, cold salad, buns and twenty beer cases and two dozen bottles of rum. On the bed, placed together was the clothing they would wear that night.

Felicita's mother took ill and died a year later. Then her father and brother moved to a smaller apartment because, as things stood, the house was overwhelming them.

The parents of Robertico no longer took part in official events and kept away from the press. They divided up the insurance money into equal parts. It was the first time they agreed on anything without arguing.

Emilia, Bebo's wife, the flight attendant, dressed early that afternoon. She had called the airport and when she heard that the flight was delayed, her hands began to tremble. A while later she repeated the call and asked to speak to the control post. "The plane had a technical problem". There was a great commotion from their side saying that they were very busy. Emilia noted the disturbance in the voice and waited no longer. She left for the airport. "What happened to 455?" The pilot seeing his friend's wife, looking disturbed and asking that question, made him feel that she knew what happened. He embraced her and holding on to his emotionis told her: "You have to be strong".

Emilia fainted.

In Georgetown, capital of Guyana, the parents and brothers of those students were watching television when an announcer interrupted the program and gave the news report.

– This isn't George's plane, it's another one – said her mother trying to convince her husband who was rushing to the phone.

Daniel the husband of Belkys, the stewardess, to whom he was recently married, remained in Barbados for two more weeks. One hour after the catastrophe he was on a motorboat in the area where the plane had fallen to the sea. He helped to recover the remains of the plane and the passengers. In the morgue he recognized the body of a stewardess, but it was not Belkys. When he learned that Hernán and Lugo were arrested in Port of Spain he went to that neighboring island and stayed around the police station for almost forty eight hours. A Cuban official recognized him and when he asked what he was doing there Daniel answered that he was trying to get a gun to kill the two terrorists. Seeing the amazement of the diplomat he added: "Don't worry, I'll shoot myself after so as not to compromise my government."

Two days later he was sent back to Havana.

The telegram notifying the acceptance of one of the fencers in the Faculty of Journalism was left on the chest forgotten for years in the small wooden room where his mother lived.

Reading the roll call, the teacher read his name. All the students stood up and said: "Present!"

In Cuba the tragedy caused stupefaction, consternation, a feeling of horror and as the causes of the disaster were uncovered, a suffocating indignation. For several days an unending and uninterrupted line silently filed in front of the eight coffins that contained the remains of the bodies of the Cubans recovered. A solemn act in a central plaza of the city gathered about a million angry people and for three weeks the telephones of the offices of Cubana de Aviación didn't stop wringing with condolences for the family of the victims, some who never recovered from the tragedy. The father of one of the dead fencers refused to accept the news and remained in the airport for a week awaiting the arrival of his daughter. "Some may say I've gone crazy – he confessed to a journalist – but I wish I really were crazy to believe in my fantasy. Then I'll see her disembark."

Rotman looked at the wall clock and understood that the pilots of Cubana were about to fulfill the five minutes since the report of the fire aboard. But they needed three minutes to touch down.

He realized that if a miracle didn't happen that plane would unavoidable crash.

– Sea landing – he said to himself and shuddered.

He pressed to talk button of the mike and tried to relieve the dramatic tension in the command cabin of CU–455 saying:

– CU–455 we have a complete emergency and continue hearing you.

– If they had delayed five minutes in taking flight ...

The manager of the Cuban airline, who heard what Rotman said, looked at him in bewilderment.

Several days later, he would explain his words:

– The plane, due to the direction of the wind, rose in the opposite direction of its destination, Jamaica. Then he made a pronounced turn of one hundred eighty degrees, a maneuver that prevented him from reaching height rapidly. Situating himself in the 315–385 radials he rose at three thousand feet a minute. If he had taken off five minutes later the explosion would have occurred at three thousand feet altitude and about twelve miles from the airport and not at a height of eighteen thousand feet and twenty eight miles distance. He would only need about three minutes to return.

Another thing that Rotman didn't realize at the time and which he thought about many times is that, also, if they had taken off only five minutes later the depressurization caused by the opening in the fuselage would not have released the oxygen masks at three thousand feet altitude since at that height their use is at the discretion of the captain. Knowing about the fire on board he would not have set it in function to prevent the oxygen from contribute to the rapid propagation of the flames; even the crew, using the extinguishers could have put the fire out.

– "Yes he commented many times when referring to that afternoon – They only needed five minutes. But those children were anxious to get home."

He stood in front of the face of the stewardess. She was very pale and her hands were around her throat and then he understood that she had died of suffocation.

He took out the photograph of his daughter and wife from his billfold and looked at them for a while. Now his face seemed calm and at rest. His white skin had become a dirty gray. He was covered in soot. He coughed several times.

He looked so vulnerable that, under the look of that generous man, it seemed that that terrifying reality had dissipated.

A fire blow made the door creak.

Bebo closed his eyes and rested his back and head against the toilet fixtures, he took another breath and let fall the empty tank. His eyes were half closed but his eyes couldn't be seen. His muscles were relaxing and he thought of the little girl at his side and she caressed his hair.

His arms and face were burned and the rest of the body was hot and covered by soot. A cloud of lethal smoke descended and covered his body. His vision clouded and he felt an unbearable pressure in his head. Suddenly his sphincters relaxed and he wet himself. He lay down and lifted his knee to his chest; he curled up, opened his mouth and died.

In the next bathroom, Irene felt coldness in that inferno. A Guyanese student who sought protection there pressed the faucet of the water basin. She swallowed some water catching it in her hands opened like a flower; with his free hand the Guyanese wet her face. Later he helped her to sit on the toilet and knelt covering the cracks under the door with newspapers in an attempt to stop the smoke.

For a few minutes Irene felt better; at least she stopped coughing. Somehow the some decontaminated air entered her lungs. The sight of the boy, who stayed at her side, kneeling very close in that narrow toilet, boosted her spirits. She wanted to talk to him but assumed he wouldn't understand her.

– I'm going to study medicine – he said in perfect Spanish and tried to smile but his smile vanished at once.

– I'm going to have a baby – she told him and began to cry while she pressed her stomach.

About thirty centimeter from her body, in the waste compartment was about to explode.

Wilfredo trembled, perspired while he blinked furiously holding on to the rudder. He could hear his own breathing like an animal caught in a trap.

Smoke kept filtering into the cabin and although the masks supplied oxygen it was unavoidable that some of the toxic emanations pass to the lungs of the three men.

The screams from the passenger section had stopped.

The copilot took with his eyes totally opened the microphone and pressed the carrier again and shouted:

– We're burning fiercely!

The message was not received by the control tower because the plane was at very low altitude but it was registered by the pilots of the Cariwest DQ–650 that was flying over that zone at a greater height.

At that moment the nose of the Cuban plane pointed up to the sky. The copilot, panicking feeling the end near, looked at the captain holding on to the rudder. The tail cables had just burst as a result of the second explosion, the one in the toilet. The copilot misunderstood that Wilfredo was trying to gain height. That is why he shouted:

– That is worse, Felo! Take to the water, Felo! Take to the water!

Rotman shuddered when he heard that voice whose horrific sounds he will never forget for the rest of his life.

Wilfredo was clutching the rudder like someone falling from a high building holds his glasses to prevent them from breaking. His eyes were terribly opened.

Then he felt a deep calm, as if time had stopped. He understood that his life ended there, at that moment, although the worse was yet to come.

At that moment the sea appeared before his eyes.

In the yacht the tourists were gathered at the bow, watching the unusual flight of that plane that was issuing smoke from the wing and tail.

They saw it raise its nose to the sky, seeming to stand still in the air and totally stop. Then it leaned over its right wing and fell.

– Cubana this is Cariwest 650. Can we help you in something?

Rotman heard in silence. He knew that the DQ–650 was flying at that moment at five thousand feet of altitude above the zone where Cubana should be.

– Cubana this is Cariwest 650. Can we help you in something?

Again silence. Rotman lowered his head.

The yacht approached. The waters were covered with masses of human flesh. Amidst the remains of the plane and baggage: a red cap with a silver plane on the brim, cassettes, baby clothes, a rattle, a doll with very open eyes, a fencing mask, seat cushions of the plane, several extinguishers, two oxygen bottles and half a dozen hand bags, all black. Like a cross, a sword stuck out of one.

On October 6, 1976, two Venezuelan terrorist hired by two others of Cuba origin, blew up a plane of the Cubana de Aviación airline in mid flight with 73 passengers on board, all civilians.

a l b e r t o   g u e r r a

For Alexis Díaz-Pimienta

SEPTEMBER ELEVEN

This story could well begin in Havana, with a hearse, in a rainy day and a sea of people in silence. Minutes before, four members of the diplomatic corps brought down the coffin down the stairs of the funeral parlor of Calzada y K, placed it carefully in the hearse, placed the crowns of flowers and everyone began the walk to the cemetery. They walked as the rain fell on their grief-stricken faces. Umbrellas could be seen here and there, groups of pioneers, puddles, uncovered heads, tears of some close friends, police stopping traffic, tears mixing with rain drops. The people in the cars, bus stops and in the buses talked of the silent march. All had heard the news: the drivers, the employees, the writers, the accountants, the housewives, the singers, the teachers, the adulterous, the office secretaries, the delinquents, the retired, the widows, the workers, the students, the leaders. Absolutely everyone had heard the news. Radio Reloj had broadcast it, also the National News Station, *Granma* and *Juventud Rebelde*. The old newspaper vendors shouted the news: Felix García is dead. As simple as that, with just four words This Story could well begin in Havana, with a hearse, under a rainy day and a sea of people in silence Minutes before, four members of the diplomatic corps lowering the coffin down the stairs of the funeral parlor, Calzada y K, placing it very carefully in the hearse, placing the crowns of flowers and all walking to the cemetery. They walked while the rain fell on their grief–stricken faces. There were umbrellas open, groups of pioneers, puddles, uncovered heads, the tears of the close friends and family, police stopping traffic, tears mixing with raindrops. The people in cars, in the bus stops, in the buses, everyone commented on the silent march. All had heard the news: the drivers, employees, writers, accountants, housewives, singers, the teachers, the adulterous, the office secretaries, the delinquents, the retired, the widows, the workers, the students, the leaders. Absolutely everyone had heard the news. Radio Reloj had transmitted it, also the National News Station, *Granma* and *Juventud Rebelde*; the old newspaper vendors shouted the news: Felix García is dead. As easy as that, with only four words, the news spread by word of mouth. Félix García is dead. In truth, few knew who Félix García was, but everyone bought the papers, read about it, made comments, shared the news and later joined the walk behind the hearse. They knew he wasn't a famous man to be remembered, he had not broken any world record in sports, he was not a singer–songwriter with long hair and a guitar, nor a politician who often gave interviews to the press. They had just learned of his existence because of his death. An unbelievable death. A disturbing death. An unusual death. Félix García, with such a common name and common surname that could have been anyone of them; that is why they joined the march as the hearse moved forward; they cried under the rain, walked in silence and forever placed the name of the unknown man in a place where the collective memory could not forget.

An hour later, still under the rain, in the farewell speech at the grave site the vice president of the country, moved, warned his compatriots, the people and international public opinion that the death of Comrade Félix García would not go unpunished, that he will continue to be with the people who saw him born; that those who committed the affront, sooner than later, will pay and that September 11, date of the criminal action would be, in the future, the day to commemorate our diplomats fallen in the foreign service.

Such a beginning, however, would sow a dismal patina in the readers, of rain and tears, of burial and coffin that I have found removes the personage from his real self because, for his colleagues, Félix García was always a happy man, with his thoughts on the many situations of life.

I prefer, then, to hear an alarm clock ring, a simple alarm clock on a simple night table and that his hand, the hand of Felix, slip out from under the sheets to shut it off as always and steal a few more minutes of sleep. A beginning like this, less dramatic, more natural, more human will let you and I see him sitting in bed, ready to light the lamp, stretch his arms, such a large yawn as possible in the solitude of the room and look at the floor. He can't find his slippers, only his moccasins are there with the socks in them; on a chair beyond his trousers next to the sweater, the shirt and coat. Disasters of a single man, he says. If I were a movie director that would be the title of my first film. I'm a mess. Lowering his head he tries to find the damned slippers, he feels around drowsily and finds one. He gets up, stretches, well we don't have to exaggerate he continues saying. No one still complains of my little oversights. He turns on the radio. He walks slowly about the room. The voice of the broadcaster, in a fast English says that New York is the best city of the free world, a free world where I can't find the other slipper, he thinks, while she announces *Saturday Night Fever*, the film's song that every one wants to see, sung and danced by a young successful man called Travolta and at the other side of the bed, at last, he finds the lost slipper. He moves on to the bathroom. I have a busy day today, he says, go to the airport, pick up the passages, pass by the post office, go to America House and meet with the foreign minister. I will first go to America House and later to the airport. No. Well. I'll decide later what to do. What I cannot do is forget the meeting with the foreign minister. Oh yes, I have to pass by the dry cleaners. I haven't any clean clothing. A hard day. He tries to urinate, nothing better than urinating warmly in the morning when you have lived in New York for a long time and when you have watched through the window, the coldness of the streets chock full of cars and people in a hurry, he thinks, but ends up seated on the toilet. He places his elbows on his knees, puts his head in his hands and looks around for a long while. He stretches his hand and reaches for a *Bohemia*. He looks at the cover with a picture of Juantorena and imagines the public in the stadium applauding the track champion. He applauds and looks at the rest of his sports mates happily. The people in the stadium are shouting excitedly. Juantorena sits, tired and the cameras continue to follow him. It is the power of imagination. Nothing more potent in any man than the imagination. However, in that very New York, not far from there that he has no idea, another man, with his pants

149

down and a nasty face is also sitting in the toilet, but with a difference: he has a terrible stomachache.

Shit, the man thinks, this always happens to me. Probably nerves. Every time there's a problem, I get loose. I finish, sweating, wash my hands and he wets his neck and slowly puts on his glasses, fills a glass, looks in the mirror and discovers a man with small eyes behind the glasses, he gulps the water in the glass like a palliative for the immediate future that he has called a mess. He dries his hands but leaves his face wet. He leaves the bathroom at the same time, Félix does the same, neither imagining it.

In his room, with the moccasins in reach, the Cuban diplomat places his hands on his waist and begins the first of the day's great missions: his exercises. One, two, three, first turning the neck to the right, to the left, to the right, to the left, one, two three, then the shoulders, one two three, the arms, one two three, the forearms, one two three, in the legs the muscles don't develop like in the other parts of the body, one, two, one two, luckily men use trousers, one, two, one, two, luckily the shinbones aren't in view, one two.

The other one, on the contrary, offers the impression of not liking exercises, he just places his hands on his stomach when the others are watching and he sits close to the fat man who is drumming his fingers on his legs while he talks to six people as if he were weaving a speech to a large audience. The fat man looks hard at the glasses, smiles sarcastically, changes the tone of his voice "Every time there is a "fiesta" you run to the bathroom, pal. The others laugh. The man with the glasses expecting the affront, talks back: Leave that alone, you know that there is no fear in this body; probably last night's shrimp upset my stomach. Then the fat man calls for silence, enthusiastic, recovers his previous tone of voice, stands up and starts walking around the room. Categorically he says, that's the way I like it, pal, that's it, he looks at everyone, sighs and declares that with people like them there can be no fear, that today would be a great day for the cause, that the whole world would always remember March 24, that among professionals who fight for freedom there can be no weakness, he expected that the photographs were already burned together with the rest of the papers because with such an important operation the first thing was to burn the evidence that would serve against the group, that this thing was cleared up last night, that they had spent six months organizing that action, six months watching the guy, twenty four hours, every day, for six months, taking his picture when he walked in, photographs when he leaves, time of entering, time of going out and now, at the last moment nothing could fail, that before leaving he was going to review the plan to make everything clear ...

Twenty-six, twenty-seven, twenty-eight. Félix tries to do the right number of push–ups, twenty nine, thirty that keep him in form, thirty three, thirty four, the ones that keep his chest in the same form, forty two, forty three, just right for his suit, sixty, sixty one, eighty three, to demonstrate that New York is the best city in the free world, ninety, ninety one, the city that wishes its inhabitants the best of mornings, ninety three, ninety four, even though the cold winter doesn't let you walk around in shirtsleeves, with light clothing through the streets, ninety five and perspiration drops on the floor, ninety six, close to the moccasins, ninety seven, not imagining, unable to imagine, that not too far away, ninety eight, in another room, ninety nine, a fat mans weaves his speech, one hundred, one hundred push-ups before a group of only six persons.

...Because the Homeland needs actions like these to rid it of communism, the fat man says and is pleased for how well the phrase turned out, a shame that the group is so small, we are only seven, seven cats, but it is better this way, the fewer, the more bread and glory, another good phrase but I can't say it. Look men, I repeat the plan, that its getting late; the driver arrives to pick up the man, he parks in front, gets out as always for a coffee with the guard then our truck arrives in the street, hiding their view; I use this cover to stick the material under the diplomatic car then you (pointing to the man with the glasses) with wide open eyes wait for them to get in, we follow them and when they are on Franklin Delano Roosevelt Drive (he again points to the man with the glasses) you press the button and bam, *adiós muchachos, compañeros de mi vida[1]* . Then we get out, everyone knows where and I call the press. Any question?

Perspiring, Félix looks at the alarm clock. Time for a good bath, he thinks. Time for a good bath and to go out into the world. But before, he opens the drawer and looks for his agenda, checks the date of the next cultural activity in the America House and puts it back. Then he sees the gun, picks it up, looks at it for a few moments, puts it back in the greased

---

[1] A tango that is about bidding farewell to friends.

nylon, as if it were a museum piece and says to himself: No matter how much I want to, girl, I can't take you out for a walk along the city, it's better for you to continue to live like this, wrapped up. He puts it back, gets up, whistles to the music on the radio and goes to the bathroom. The hot shower cleanses the perspiration in his body. Félix whistles, Félix sings, Félix thinks of his aunt Eva while he soaps up. Hell, its been a long time since I've gone over there. You're needing a first class rice and chicken, you bachelor. When I get a chance, I'll call her and take her a magazine.

The car with the diplomatic plates parks in front of the residence of the Cuban ambassador to the United Nations. The street, crammed with cars, leaves little space to park. Some cars stop, drop off some young people who barely say good-bye and then move on. The young people greet each other, some go into the school but others, most of them, prefer to hang around in the area while they still have time. The driver of the diplomatic car looks towards the entrance of the residence and doesn't see anyone at the door. Then he looks at his watch. It is still too early. The guard looks out. Makes signs to him. The driver understands. A sip of Cuban coffee. Nothing like a good cup of coffee. The chauffer gets out and leaves the motor running and walks to the entrance. Before, he looks back a few times. He goes in. The truck belonging to Losada Fernández, according to the signs, appears at the corner moving fast, stops for a moment in front of the ambassador's residence. The best moment for the fat man to crouch down, not being seen, like a snake in a jungle of cars and attach the bomb under the gas tank. Everything is perfect. Just like they wanted. Now, all they had to do was wait for the return of the driver still tasting the last coffee in his life, with Raúl Roa Kourí, Cuban ambassador to the UN.

Both leave the residence. The Cuban guard as always, watches them leave, never thinking that the man with the glasses next to the fat man sitting a few meters away with a detonator in his hand has been watching them leave for six months, but for a different reason: they want March 25 to be the last time. They wait for the car to move out, to arrive at Franklin Delano Roosevelt Drive, for them to feel confident in the middle of the road and when they least expect it: Bam. It's just a matter of time.

The diplomatic car tries to move between so many cars. A difficult maneuver. Come on, get a move on. The man with the glasses is perspiring because of the shrimp he ate last night, but the fat man, although he doesn't eat shrimp, is perspiring profusely also. Come on, move out. The driver maneuvers unwittingly on the way to death. The Cuban ambassador to the United Nations observes the maneuver, accustomed to New York streets filled with cars, but his thoughts are far from there. Come on, get out. The guard begins to light a one sixty Popular that the driver just gave him. Come on, lets move out. The fat man drums his fingers on the wheel. The man with the glasses doesn't want to think of the shrimp in sauce. Come on, get a move on. At last, the driver, turning the wheel as hard as he can, being extra careful, manages to get out, not before hitting the car in front. It stumbles and something falls. What was that? The ambassador asks. What was that? The car with the diplomatic plates stops after a few minutes. The guard runs over. The driver gets out. The man with the glasses has the detonator in his hands. It all depends on his hands. Hit it now, the fat man shouts. This looks like a bomb, the guard says. The driver says a bomb. Get a move on, they are near, hit it right here. No. Hit it, shit. No, there are children about. Shit. Goddamn kids nearby. The driver runs to the ambassador. Get out of the car, they placed a bomb. The ambassador walks with the driver towards the residence. He calls our people right away. The guard nervously placed the bomb in a dumpster. And call the police. Let's get out of here, the fat man shouts. The guard runs towards the residence. Protect the women and children. Another guard of the neighborhood watches as the custodian throws something strange into the closest dumpster. He walks down and sees the object. He takes it and, without thinking, walks rapidly to a farther corner, reaching another dumpster, and looking in both directions, throws it in. The fat man and the man with the glasses argue. Things didn't turn out well at the last minute, damn it. Six months of planning. Where is the bomb? asks Néstor García, the representative of the Cuban Mission to the United Nations. I put it in the dumpster, the guard tells him.

Let's go see. Several police cars arrive. But there is nothing there. What's the matter with you? the other guard asks. There was a bomb here. A bomb? Yes a bomb. I put it in the other dumpster over there. They all run. When they reach it, the bomb isn't there either. Where can the damn bomb be? Someone got to it but, who? The garbage truck is in the other block, emptying the dumpsters automatically after three workers check them out. The garbage collectors. The garbage collectors have it. Néstor runs, the two guards run. The police run. The man with the glasses gets out and wants to ask what happens, to be sure of the failure with his own eyes. What happened here? It seems that they put a bomb, a schoolteacher explains. The man with the glasses goes back to the fat man. We're off. Néstor, the guards and the police run. The garbage truck is getting ready to leave. They arrive just in time. I need you to return this, Néstor tells the garbage driver. Now way bud, he answers. I need it now. No way, the driver answers from the cabin plastered in naked women. We saw it first and that is the law in any city, foreigner. And if I told you it is a bomb. A bomb? Yes. You will have to prove it. Put it there, Nestor points to the truck cabin. The driver is surprised because it is magnetized and is stuck to the breast on one of those pinups. He gets out real fast. A bomb, a bomb, he shouts and runs, runs and shouts, with the workers, moving as far away as he can from the truck.

On the afternoon of September 11, barely six months after the terrible failed attempt against the Cuban foreign minister, the diplomat, Felix García was far from imagining that he would be involved in another mortal incident. Invited, as so many times before for dinner in the house of aunt Eva, he would first pass by the Mission to pick up the wife and daughters of Néstor García (there's a reason for having the same surname, Félix told the attaché this morning), but when he arrived (forgive me, I got mixed up in the airport), he found Néstor to take them himself: don't worry Félix, we'll wait for you at aunt Eva's and don't delay, there's rice and chicken announced.

The fat man and the one with glasses, had just lain in wait near the diplomatic mission, after having lost the trail of a couple of Cuban officials, according what the man with the glasses said a few months later to the FBI detective working on the case. We were frustrated, he said, everything was going wrong and something had to be done. They saw Félix go out, alone in the car. Come on, let's follow him, the fat man said, that this lower official will lead us to the big ones. We might even find the foreign minister himself.

Felix García realized that he was being followed when he entered the garage. Then he decided not to go directly to the house of aunt Eva, at least not until he lost them. He had already gone by the dry cleaners, had already given a couple of *Bohemia* to the owners and had changed in the dry cleaners to save time. Come on boy, show me the way, the fat man repeated while he waited for the Felix's eight-cylinder Ford station wagon to leave the garage. Things couldn't keep on turning out bad for the group. No one would give them credit. No one would give a penny for the cause. Everything was one failure after another, he thought. The bomb for Castro in New York last year was a failure. The one for the foreign minister another failure. It's not enough with introducing hemorrhagic Dengue in Cuba, something that makes this stupid bastard too proud (he looks at the man with glasses with revulsion). No, other hits are needed, blood must flow, panic felt, make it difficult for them to get out, that the communists and their sympathizers learn that the struggle is no game. Come on, boy, take us to the cheese. Come on.

Félix García began zigzagging in the streets of New York trying to lose them. He couldn't lead them to the house of aunt Eva's and he didn't want to return to the mission; it was just a question of losing them, to quickly turn a corner, like they do in the movies. That September 11 he was far from imagining that his life would end. That morning, with several Chilean colleagues he had commemorated the resistance of President Salvador Allende, before the terrorist coup by Pinochet and, now, in the afternoon, the Ford with the diplomatic plates was very close to the huge twin towers. It was not the first time he was followed. To persecute and insult was a juicy business for some. Felix looked at the magazines, looked at the files, drummed his fingers on the wheel when his car was stopped by a red light. He also remembered that he should have had his gun near, the girl with whom he shared his trips along the city preferred to have it in the drawer, greased, like a museum piece and not an object of death. They he felt the car hit, that something was shouted, he lowered the window. Damn you, shitty worm, he answered, the best possible shouts and only saw a gun aiming at him.

Jagüey Grande, July 2002

This was the first assassination in the United States of a diplomat accredited to the United Nations, on September 11, 1980.

adelaida fernández de juan

To the mothers of over a hundred
children who died of dengue in 1981,
and to all health workers

THE DAUGHTER OF DARIO

Maria Eugenia was on her night shift in the hospital when the telephone from the intensive care ward rang. She answered in her usual calm manner. She was used to the gravity of almost everything. The unexpected improvement of a patient in critical condition was not strange for her or if a not so sick patient, was dead by dawn, or to be more exact, if that patient did not awake in one of her shifts.

Four times a week she covered the night shift. Although for many years she expressed her preference to work at night, now, forty-five years old, no one believed that her daughter, about to be eleven, could need so much day care as she claimed.

Nonetheless, early mornings are so gloomy in hospitals that the other nurses thought it convenient (curious but convenient) to have Maria Eugenia insist on "doing the early dawn hours" over and over again.

Eleven years before, (no one remembered), an engineer who was supervising of the sugar mill, had arrived from Havana to the town hospital and Maria Eugenia was the one to attend him.

—I'm a bit agitated —he said —. Can you please give me an aerosol?

—Right away—she said. —But we don't say "agitated" here, we say "tired".

—I really don't care how it's said. You do understand that I have asthma, no?

—Of course, engineer, relax, you'll soon feel better, you'll see.

—And how do you know that I am an engineer?

—Ah… —and she gave him the nozzle connected to the oxygen tank—. Because you look like an engineer and you're not from here. No…don't talk, keep breathing the vapor.

It's not that that night was special, with more stars or hotter than others, nor was the bagasse dust dirtying her white nurse's uniform. It wasn't even carnival night. Rather, it was a boring night and, perhaps, that is why the engineer, when relieved, stayed with Maria Eugenia until the sun came up and the mill whistle blew announcing that the town was coming to life again. She changed rapidly in the nurse's locker, still not believing every thing that had happened. To be more exact, not believing that she had allowed it to happen.

—I'm going back to Havana today —he said—. I'll call you one of these nights.

The B. Sc. in Intensive Care offered in the capital of the province was just right for Maria Eugenia. Her impeccable dossier, her acknowledged dedication, her skill and, also, her early pregnancy, made her the perfect candidate for the course.

She returned a year and a half later describing the magnificence of the provincial hospital, talking of the museums, culture houses, hotels, showing the neighbors the baby girl she had had there, of whose father she had gotten a divorce right away.

Several times, she was offered trips to Havana for National Nurse's Meetings and she refused them every time claiming that it was more than enough that her neighbors were willing to watch after her little girl while she was at work so as to also, ask them to care for her if she was in Havana.

However, after thinking it over for a long time (the dawns, in addition to being gloomy are ideal for meditation) she came to the conclusion that eleven years were enough to start understanding some things. And when he called "*one of these nights*" as he had said, she would tell him about the little girl, she would talk to her about him regardless of how many other children he had, she (Maria Eugenia) was going to tell her that it was time to go to Havana.

That she wanted to have ice cream in Coppelia, chamomile in the Casa del Te, eat *medias noches*[1] in the Carmelo de 23, take her picture in front of the Capitol, sit on the lions of Prado, see a film in Yara. She wanted her little girl to know of Silvio Rodríguez, Pablo Milanés, to breathe the salty sea mist of the Malecón, she wanted her to shout his name in the gazebo of the park in 21st street, to hear the echo return it and all these marvels he told her about the night he had come feeling agitated (actually tired).

That is what Maria Eugenia wanted to tell her. In truth, she kept adding demands every dawn and leaving out some of the first ones. For example, she no longer thought it a good idea, as she did at the beginning, to tell her daughter who her father was. Too traumatic and useless.

Every time summer vacations came, Maria Eugenia would say, in passing, *maybe we'll go to Havana this year* and also, in passing, she would describe the memories of the unknown places to the little girl.

They say that the Yara, called Radiocentro before, shows beautiful films.

And the following year:

They once told me that the Carmelo de 23 was a very elegant cafeteria and that it is on a great avenue called 23.

And the next:

You'll love Coppelia. It's a gigantic ice cream parlor, with many aisles and a central staircase.

The night the telephone rang, Maria Eugenia answered with her customary equanimity and she thought she heard:

It's me Dario. I want you to come to Havana. I'll be waiting at the train station next Sunday.

She felt all the fear in the world (that's what she thought then). She didn't talk of specific wishes to visit a special place, or of drinks, nor ice cream, or of the photographs she planned about for almost eleven years, nor, the worst, did she talk of her daughter. She waited for daybreak, asked for sixty days vacations, *yes ... consecutives ... I'll double shifts*

---

[1] Typical sweet bread sandwich that was very popular in Cuba, filled with slices of ham, pork, sweet pickled gherkins, mayonnaise and mustard.

later ... yes, it's an emergency ... yes, of course I'll come back, and she ran to the train station, bought two tickets and picked up her little girl.

She had sixteen hours to talk to her and, although she was still sure it was not a good idea to tell her that the man who would meet them in Havana, was her father, there were moments, for example, between Cacocum and Las Tunas, when she doubted.

Reading the long itinerary, according to the listing of towns and cities in the map she had bought once, just in case, she made mental note of how many things she and her daughter could talk about before getting off in Havana.

Reaching Hatuey, she described again the taste of orange pineapple ice cream in Coppelia that was different from the pineapple glacé. It had an added light orange flavor.

During the stretch through Siboney, Camagüey and Florida, they talked of the main avenues in Havana. The little girl added details that Maria Eugenia had forgotten and they laughed over the confusion of mistaking the Paseo del Prado for the Avenida de los Presidentes, the grand L street where the Yara theater is (they said), Linea where the train used to pass and so on until they fell asleep.

When the Santa Clara station was announced, Maria Eugenia woke up and, although she felt that suddenly it was hot in the train, she drifted off thinking of the happiness awaiting them.

The train cars were filled with young boys and girls who, since it was July, were going to Havana for holidays, more or less, as they were too.

Passing Limonar, just before Matanzas, they began the tour in their minds, that from so much wishing, they already knew:

—Walking along the Avenida de los Presidentes, you reach Carmelo de 23, that has two parts —Maria Eugenia said—: the part outside is the cafeteria, where you can order the *medias noches* and the inside is the real restaurant with air conditioning and everything else.

—And there won't be *medias noches* inside? —the little girl asked.

—I don't think so, but we'll find out ourselves.

It was in Aguacate (they didn't talk in Matanzas, The child was sleepy again and drowsed off, in the sleepiness typical of trains) and Maria Eugenia again noted that there was too much heat. Not that she was hot, but that the

160

train temperature was unusually hot. Arriving at Havana, the child was still drowsy and when her mother shook her, she sat up to look out the windows.

—Isn't it beautiful, my love? —Maria Eugenia asked without paying much attention, looking for Darío. The Darío she remembered from a long and ancient night, to be exact.

Several passengers began to vomit when they got off the train, a strange atmosphere enveloped the station. Many of the children who had traveled from the eastern and central provinces, couldn't wake up completely and the mothers, at first wondering and later getting alarmed began to ask for help from the station workers, among the rest of the passengers and finally shouted for help.

Maria Eugenia left the girl in charge of their suitcases and, with her training in intensive care she went to aid those who seemed more lethargic. The physicians of the train station accepted her help and, equally stunned, started applying dextrose or saline solution drips or any other intravenous solutions available in the medical post.

They had never calculated so many emergencies at the same time. While some could not stop vomiting, others mumbled that they felt their life slipping away, all with fevers, complaining. The children, in their mothers' arms, cried in fright, asking to go back home.

The station benches became improvised stretchers. Surrounding traffic was stopped and without taking time to write down names or addresses, they moved everyone in the cars of people who had gone to receive someone.

Among the crowd of people who became stretcher–bearers or para-medics (impossible to know who was doing so officially and who voluntarily) Maria Eugenia thought she saw Darío. It was when the station chief used the loudspeakers to ask people to stay calm, that ambulances were on the way, *that the children would be taken to the Centro Habana Children's Hospital ... the adults would go to the Calixto García ... please, everyone should remember their identity card ... the ambulances are arriving ...*

Maria Eugenia, in the station crowd, amidst the noise and confusion, forgot where she thought she had seen Darío. She ran to the spot where her daughter was and only found the suitcases. She ran over all the obstacles in her mad dash, jumping over benches, calling out her daughter's name.

All the fear of the world came upon her (she felt) and, without knowing who to ask for help, went to the exit where the ambulances were arriving.

Again she thought she saw Darío. What's more, it seemed that Darío was looking at her. To be more exact, it seemed that Darío thought that he was looking at her, but it was at that precise moment that the first ambulance siren announced its departure. Maria Eugenia only managed to ask the driver if she could check if her daughter was there, in one of the stretchers at the back.

The normal division of the wards according to disease of the pediatric hospital had to be ignored. Once all the wards were filled, the physicians and nurses placed beds in the corridors, in the waiting rooms, in the treatment cubicles, everywhere where they could place a drip stand.

Maria Eugenia recognized some mothers who were on the train and the children who, like her daughter, were coming to the city of dreams for the first time. Although she was deeply depressed, she tried to raise the spirits of the rest and, in spite of the lethargy her daughter was in, she took charge of checking all the drips in the ward. The ward nurse had been on duty for forty-eight hours so she was grateful to be able to sit a while on the stairs. Maria Eugenia checked each and every bed with children from the provinces and Havana. She'd give hope to the mothers in the hope of feeling hope herself and without letting the rest of them know, she asked the doctors for hope, the doctors who never stopped going from one bed to another in the desperate attempt to save the children who were dying or who died in a matter of minutes.

The nurse who had gone to sit on the stairs for a while was the one who notified her. The girl was being taken to the intensive care ward because it was impossible to control the bleeding that had started in the vein puncture.

Maria Eugenia tried to behave with her customary equanimity, with the professionalism of many years of experience, with the severity that corresponds to a single mother, with the composure required in one of the most demanding professions of the world; but all the fear of the world enveloped her (now definitely) and she refused to let them take her daughter in the stretcher like all the rest.

She carried the child herself, holding her close to her breast and fled with her to the waiting physicians and nurses, as exhausted as everyone else.

She was not prepared to hear the words that she had pronounced so often, *we did everything possible,* or similar phrases, knowing that these did not offer any comfort. So she went in with her daughter, helped intubate her and, with them all, helped to place the artificial respirator, she helped them find a vein that would resist and when they all embraced her, because it had been in vain, Maria Eugenia thought she saw Darío.

Through the glass of the intensive therapy ward, she finally held his gaze because she was no longer interested in Coppelia, or Carmelo, or El Prado, or the large streets. What's more, she was not even interested in love. Because she was no longer interested in anything at all.

In 1981 there was a dengue epidemic in Cuba that, in a few weeks, cost the lives of 158 persons; 101 were children and the disease affected 344 203 persons. The first cases appeared simultaneously in different localities of the Island, more than 300 Km apart. There was no epidemiological explanation to identify the epidemic like a natural infection. The sudden appearance, with no known epidemic in the American region, nor in any of the countries with which Cuba maintained important exchanges of persons, and its simultaneous appearance in different regions of the country, were points of departure for the studies done by prestigious Cuban scientists in cooperation with highly qualified scientists from other countries who were specialized in the detection and struggle against biologic aggressions. Months later, during a court trial in New York, against a terrorist of Cuban origin resident in New York, Eduardo Arozena, this individual confessed that he had introduced the hemorrhagic dengue virus in Cuba.

jesús david curbelo

For Manuel Mendive

THE PHOENIX

Maferefún, Ochún Funké, the Maestro said and introduced the brush into the deep yellow of the palette. Maferefún, Yemayá Yalode, he said and dipped it in navy blue. Maferefún, Changó and the red nourished the canvas' thirst. Maferefún, Ogún and he added the green of the woodlands. They blended with the black of Eleguá Alaroye who already lived in the drawing of the bird that kissed the breasts of the dancing females, cutting their figures from the white background that Obatalá gave them since the origins of the world. The bodies were gradually filled with the previous desiree of the flesh, a desire that beat forever in the spirit of El Maestro. His hand, instrument of Olofi to breath and give life to those beings returned once and again to the canvas with the erotic precision of a goldsmith who polishes the stone until releasing its sparkle of love. That is what it was all about, of love, happiness, harmony; to erase in the delirium of the Creation that is creation, any sign of resentment, of hate, of fear, because, after all, only love gives birth to melodies. And music, the Maestro thought, is the sublime expression of the existence of the gods.

The man entered the Habana Gallery intending to buy a piece as a gift for his wife. He carefully looked at the exhibition: Mariano, Portocarrero, Servando,

165

Amelia, silk screen prints of the classics of Cuban painting at truly reasonable prices. He though of his wife: naked, beautiful and wanted something to remember her always. Then he discovered the dancers kissing the peacock. Manuel Mendive, he read. I'll buy it. He was sure his wife would love it.

Sure enough, she loved it. The painting was in exhibition in the hall for several months, receiving the praise of some and the reluctance of others confronted by the scandal of the mulattas frolicking with the bird in a dance of highly charged eroticism. Like my wife, the man thought. And it was true: he caught her one afternoon in bed with the neighbor. He later learned that he had not been the only one and the man was on the verge of going crazy. In one of his sudden attacks he thought of destroying the painting. A friend prevented it. Don't be silly, he said, there are many who would buy it at a good price.

Like someone shedding an unbearable burden, the man sold the peacock. Later he felt relieved.

For the Maestro, painting peacocks was an obsession. More than an obsession, a ceremony. The peacock, symbol of love and happiness in the Regla de Ocha was one of the attributes of Ochún and Yemayá, the dancing goddesses of the sea and rivers, the women who drove all the males of the pantheon crazy. The bird in itself, for its beauty, had always been associated with the gods; there it was, to confirm it, the iranio-sufi myth that God when creating the spirit of the world placed it in the image of the peacock and the bird, looking at the greatness he saw in the mirror released drops of perspiration creating the other beings. For the Greeks it was the sacred bird of Hera and the ovals in its tail were identified as the eyes of Argos and should protect Io, the cow of the moon. In ancient Egypt it was associated with the sun, worshiped in the temple of Heliopolis. Several traditions in India and Asia incorporated the peacock in sun motifs giving it attributes of abundance, fertility and immortality. It also appeared in Christian iconography drinking from the cup of the Eucharist, pecking the fruit of the vine or guarding the tree of life in Paradise. And the Maestro, with the universal wisdom that bestows talent, constantly painted peacocks with the certainty that he was entering the ministry of existence and giving testimony of his joy for being at peace with his ancestors.

166

– Five thousand dollars once, five thousand dollars twice and five thousand dollars thrice – the auctioneered shouted –. Sold the painting by Victor Manuel to that gentleman for five thousand dollars.

A murmur of admiration was heard among the multitude that filled the Cuban Museum in Miami.

– And now – the auctioneer began again -, we continue with our auction of Cuban art with a piece by Eduardo Abela, one of the most well known vanguard painters. It starts off at a price of five hundred dollars.

The bidding was long and tense. Several persons wanted the canvas. An opportunity such as this was quite rare. In fact, it was the second time in years. And in spite of the strong protest from some sectors accusing the museum of doing business with painters who went along with Fidel Castro and participated in the dark political culture that his government had set up in the Island. During the days before the public auction, letters charging the board of the museum circulated by the media in Miami and even a group of émigré artists appeared to protest and demand the resignation of the Board of Directors that had given green light to the presence of these works in the city.

The Abela was sold for three thousand two hundred dollars and the auctioneer then announced the next one: Portocarrero. After another bidding contest a lady obtained it for four thousand eight hundred dollars. And the auction continued: Amelia, Servando, Carmelo Gonzales and thousands of dollars were moved in the salon.

They called the Maestro right away to tell him the news. At first he didn't want to believe it. Who could think of such an atrocity? How is it possible with one iota of sensibility do such a thing? Were they sure of what they were saying? Yes, dammit, yes; it had been filmed by the television. And what could be done about that? he asked. An accusation? A lawsuit? No, a voice said on the other end of the line; in any case to feel a terrible pity for him. Perhaps, the Maestro said pensively. And later asked: Are there no more details? Some, the voice answered, but perhaps you don't want to hear them. It doesn't matter, the Maestro added, curiosity is the beginning of knowledge.

At the end of the offer the auction went on to the silk screens. That was the moment that one of the members of the group boycotting the auction, raised his card and shouted:

– One hundred fifty.

Another voice offered one hundred eighty.

The auctioneer began his singsong but did not pass to twice.

– Two hundred – the first bidder added.

–Two hundred says the gentleman – the auctioneer repeated.

–Two hundred fifty – was counter bid.

– Three hundred.

– Three hundred fifty.

– Four hundred – shocked the first bidder.

A suspicious silence invaded the hall.

The master of ceremonies answered the provocation:

– Four hundred has offered the gentleman at the back.

The looks turned to the adversary. The man kept his silence.

– Four hundred dollars once, four hundred dollars twice, four hundred dollars three – the auctioneer said excitedly –. *Ochún y el pavorreal* by Manuel Mendive sold for four hundred dollars.

It was the last piece of the night.

The new owner deposited the sum bid and lifted his trophy.

– Now you will see what these communist cartoons are good for.

Everyone looked on stunned.

The man left the museum and outside, in front of television cameras, he held the print by a corner and set fire to it with his lighter.

Everyone was too shocked to stop him.

Some just walked away disgusted. Others, smiling, shouted slogans against the Castro government.

The man dropped the flaming print and the red, green, yellow and blue flames ended up in a heap of ashes on the pavement.

The Maestro hung up.

From the window in his room he looked at the sun rising above the rooftops of Madrid.

Maferefún, Olorum, he said and greeted, also to Olodumare and Olofi.

Later he went down to his studio, prepared a new canvas, the colors on his palette and asked the blessing of his saints and began to paint.

This fascist act against culture was done by a member of the Cuban American National Foundation on April 22, 1988.

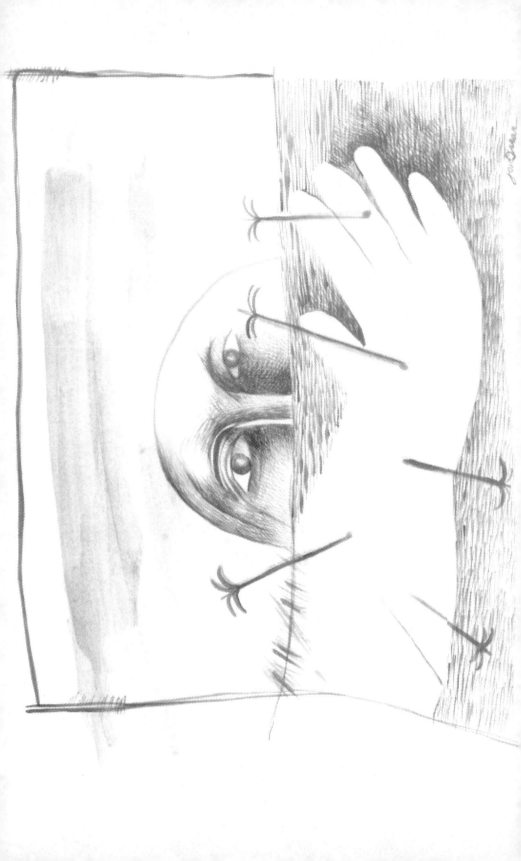

r o g e l i o   r i v e r ó n

For Emilio Comas Paret

THE NIGHT OF THE GHOSTS

So this is the pedraplén[1], H.H. said and sighed. He was nervous but tried to convince himself that this was the peak state of a warrior: *I'm not nervous, but alert*, he thought looking ahead where the coast was supposed to be; the real coast, Cuba.

They had disembarked a short time before, in the pedraplén and H.H. calculated that the mainland was about eight kilometers away. The pedraplén, a huge arm of rock, still not paved, that new tourism airs had laid to the keys north of Caibarién, offered them good cover. Whoever landed here could become a shadow, a virtual fisherman, a theater fisherman, ethereal, a quick-change artist: a lethal image that, in the dark night, could slip in with confidence towards his goal. Moreover, they had managed it: there they were.

Shortly after landing, the group split up. Of the seven on the motor boat, four had fallen behind and three decided to move forward: the Samurai, Big Truck and H.H. They moved without much precaution, escorted by the rumble of the sea against the pedraplén and the air that blew from land giving them an awkward calm, but rhythmic. In a short rest, H.H. discovered

[1]A gravel road that is used in Cuba to link keys between them and to the mainland.

the Moon. It was a thin semicircle, too yellow that night, and for some reason, reminded him of the moons of his childhood. He understood that the vision did not go easily with the optimism the breeze blew in.

—I can't see anything —Big Truck said.

—Nothing —Samurai agreed.

H.H. kept quiet.

—Do you have the irons? —Big Truck asked, just for the sake of asking. Then he sighed.

Stupid, H.H. thought, but answered:

—Of course. To burn up Cuba.

He liked the phrase since it had occurred to him in Miami, shortly before being recruited. *We will train you to infiltrate the Island*, they said. *In a few weeks you will be ready to blow it up, even the souls of your relatives*, they said. *A beast with the face of a beast*, they said. And H.H. answered: *Let's start. Burn up Cuba.*

A few days before leaving, H.H. noticed that his daughter shut herself in to read. *For some time*, he commented, *no one can take your eyes from the book*. The girl smiled. *What's that book?* H.H. wanted to find out and, since she showed him the cover, he read:

—*Moby Dick*, Herman Melville.

—You should read it —his daughter said—, I didn't know it would be so good.

H.H. made a scornful gesture in answer to the awe of his daughter. He usually read the newspapers or maybe a magazine, but not books. Without realizing it, however, he served himself a drink and picked up the book, got comfortable and began to read. Slowly, he was caught up by that fantastic duel between a man and a whale. He liked the stubbornness of Captain Ahab wanting to kill his rival. He read many pages those days, but when they told him when he was leaving, he had not yet finished the book.

H.H. decided to take Moby Dick along with him on the trip to Cuba. When the coastline disappeared over the horizon, he opened the book and tried to absorb Ahab's hatred for the beast. Later, while he was setting up the rifle and shooting at the clouds, he dreamt of Ahab and felt important: he was on the sea to search out his enemy and in search of his legend.

—We almost fucked up the fishing —the doctor said—. It rained so hard that I was afraid it would never stop.

—That's why you didn't want to come —Juan Angel said, driving—; you're the one who almost fucked it up.

Ovidio, next to the driver, listened to them. Smiling, but in silence. Caibarién, under the cloak of night and the recent rain, recovered a bit of its past arrogance and Ovidio thought that he liked his city that had no sewer system, with few trees, of a burning sun, but always willing to renovate and not accustomed to living on land. The wet lonely streets seemed like a make believe environment, very calm under the now clear sky of October and then Ovidio thought that it wasn't a bad idea to stay home that night, to take a break from fishing that he and his friends were so accustomed to.

—The night is strange —the doctor commented—, it feels like a movie mystery night.

Ovidio looked at the doctor, surprised that he mentioned an idea he had thought of a few seconds ago.

—Hey, our old buddy isn't very enthusiastic, he may ruin our fishing — Juan Angel said, pointing to him.

Ovidio smiled silently. Juan Angel kept on talking:

—I've never seen Ovidio so quite.

—It's true —the doctor added.

—I was just thinking —Ovidio explained

—Thinking … —Juan Angel poked fun at him.

—You're lost in thought today —(the doctor).

—Ever since we left —(Juan Angel).

—I think I'm not the only one who would have preferred to stay home —(the doctor).

—I see —(Juan Angel).

—Stop kidding around —(Ovidio).

There was silence, Juan Angel, at the wheel, began to laugh. "To shake the sluggishness", the doctor said and took out a bottle.

Ovidio waited his turn and took a long swallow of the home distilled rum that his friend had brought. For no apparent reason or, perhaps, because he was going out to sea, he remembered his son and a conversation they had that afternoon while he prepared his flies and lines. His son asked him about a book, *Moby Dick*. Ovidio recalled the novel. He remembered it well. because in his good times as a reader he was impressed by the tragic and enigmatic plot. But he still didn't have it. So he promised his son that he would get it for him, "I'll borrow it, steal it or rewrite it", he kidded, "but the person who recommended it was right".

—You know —the boy said— it's that they've told me that the characters in *Moby Dick* are like ghosts that are and are not and with this pushing and shoving, incredible things happen.

"Ghosts", Ovidio thought. It wouldn't have occurred to me". And admitted that *Moby Dick* was really a great book, but he, with a poet's soul, after all, preferred the whale as the main character. "Guys" he said suddenly, "I'm looking for a novel by Herman Melville: Moby Dick". Juan Angel spied him and swore. "So you come all this time in silence, as if you were angry with us and when you open your mouth it's to ask for a book, God knows from what time".

—It's for my son —Ovidio explained.

—Well, if that's the case... —(Juan Angel).

—Leave the book aside for the time being, there is the entrance of the pedraplén —(the doctor).

I stood guard over the machines of the pedraplén. In a flat area of white soil that served as the starting point, where trucks, bulldozers and all kinds of iron beasts that dripped exhaustion were parked. I also controlled the entry of fishermen. There were those who could pass, there were others who couldn't and I checked their papers and sent them on or sent them back.

That day I arrived at six. It was October and night came early. Since it had rained in the afternoon, I got ready for the mosquitoes that never failed to show up. The wind came from inland. It was a scant breeze that came in bursts, as if the sea had trouble pulling it in. I walked by the trucks with the rifle slung over my shoulder, making believe that I didn't care about the mosquitoes, that I didn't care about the twelve hours I had to stay awake, like a sleep walker in the esplanade. I was walking back and forth when a man on foot appeared. I ordered him to stop. I asked for his papers authorizing him to walk over here in the pedraplén. He answered angrily. He told me he did not have a safe-conduct that he was a man who wanted to catch a fish for his family and that he wouldn't be turned away just like that. "Well you can't continue", I assured him. If it had been day I would have seen the hatred in his eyes, but in the ghostly night I was only able to see his sudden movements and hear his angry words: "Shit. As if I needed a visa to enter here. You're an extremist. I'd stab people like you".

But he left.

I continued going along the trucks. I got in one and connected the radio. A dry old narrator invited the listeners to hear the same music as always and commented on the cold temperatures that year. I turned the radio off, got down, because a beam from Caibarién warned of an approaching car.

It was Juan Angel, Ovidio and the doctor. We knew each other from here. They fished along the pedraplén frequently and when I was on guard, we talked for a while. They told me that they had come purely by chance because the afternoon rain made them doubt.

"So much so, that we've got one who seems to be in a world of his own!" Juan Angel said laughingly looking at Ovidio. I also laughed and then the doctor added: "Today Ovidio is feeling romantic". Now, to top it off, he wants us to find a book". Since I don't know anything about books, I kept quiet when Ovidio added that the book was important, that he wanted to get it for his son who asked for it and the doctor interrupted him: "Don't worry, Ovidio, *Moby Dick* is easy to find, you'll see". Ovidio looked at me appreciatively and told Juan Angel: "Start up. Go on, that there is a bunch of fish waiting to welcome us".

H.H wanted to leave the pedraplén as soon as possible. The mission for which they were hired was many kilometers from there, in the Escambray Mountains, and if they stopped to think about it, it wasn't very clear how they would get there. *At least we're in Cuba*, Big Truck said. *If we could cross the sea, we can cross anything. We should only move by night*, Samurai explained. *Unless we can find a car.*

—And we have one—H.H. said

—What do you mean? —Big Truck asked.

Without answering, H.H. pointed behind where a couple of headlights of what seemed to be a car, appeared. Instinctively they crouched at the side of the road and kept watching the lights that had seemed to stop, while they prepared their weapons. For a few seconds, only the murmur of the sea at their backs could be heard and the soft slap of a hand trying to kill a mosquito. The car delayed in starting up again. The Samurai suggested going after it but H.H. was against it.

—It would be easy to surprise them —the Samurai insisted —. We go as quiet as wolves and fall on them.

Big Truck started to cough. *Hold that cough Big Truck*, H.H. commanded. *And you, Samurai hold your tongue and your desire to be a hero for when you are in the hills*. And he repeated the order: *wait*.

The moon was still weak and the dawn that was dry now was only a sign of monotony and those lights at a distance, like a still provocation. The Samurai was impatient but didn't want to make H.H. an enemy. Big Truck seemed undecided. In truth, he would have preferred to get rid of the feeling of *suspense* and appear like magic already in the Escambray Mountains. H.H. looked steadily at the lights. He was going to say something when he noticed they were moving. He concentrated on them more.

—It's coming —he whispered.

The Samurai jumped to the center of the pedraplén but H.H. cursing ordered him back. *Wait for my order,* he added. The minutes that followed seemed like years to Big Truck. He checked the safety of his weapon to be sure it was off, he touched the pistol in his waist and the knife he had on his leg. The lights advanced. At last, they heard the rumble of the motor and a cone of light shone on the jump made by H.H. who kneeled, pointing to the car's windshield. Ovidio, Juan Angel and the doctor, surprised saw Big Truck and Samurai, coming out of the ditch pointing their guns.

—Surprise —H.H. laughed.

—Where's this Lada from, Miami? —(Big Truck).

—Get out, slow and easy —(the Samurai)

—With your hands up —(H.H.)

—Or you die right there—(Big Truck).

They got out. The others continued to aim at them. *We have no weapons*, Ovidio said, *stop pointing at us. Careful*, H.H. shouted, *that I'll kill you and nothing will happen! We have no weapons*, Ovidio insisted. *You never know*, H.H. said with irony, *so shut up and keep your hands up*. Ovidio was going to answer and H.H. shouted something and fired. Ovidio fell at his feet. The doctor and Juan Angel jumped into the water and H.H. continued firing. The Samurai ran to him and told him to stop, *the shots can warn people*, he exclaimed excitedly.

—Get a move on— H.H. said and swore.

They got in the car and H.H. took the wheel but he couldn't start it up.

176

—See what's the matter, Big Truck —he ordered.

Big Truck started it up.

—Now we look like an army —H.H. laughed —, at least we're motorized.

I didn't hear the shots. The breeze blew toward the sea. That's why, when I saw the lights, I thought of my friends. "How soon they got bored", I said and went to receive them. The sound of the motor made me think that the Lada was moving fast. "They're probably half drunk", I guessed and since the car stopped I got close. By the dim light of the moon, I saw that someone was pointing a gun at me from the seat by the driver. Then I heard the insults and shouts to give up. I made believe that I was handing them the rifle. I slowly slipped it off and acted as if I was going to give it to them through the window, just like they demanded but I suddenly fell back. I heard the shot and started shooting from the ground, one shot after another, away from the Lada lights. They started to shout. They screamed that I had wounded them and they were giving up, but that they were many, that farther back there was a landing. "Get out, damn it", I answered.

There were three. They left their rifles in the car; since I started to shout orders, they began getting out. One attempted to approach me and I hit him in the head and left him crawling at my feet. I wanted to kick him, but I held back. As it turned out, I had wounded two. I placed them against a truck, in front of the Lada so that the car lights shone on them. "What did you do with my friends?" I said with violence. "Nothing" they insisted. "We took their car and that's all". The wound in one was just a skin wound, but the other had a hole in his arm and was moaning. "Let me take care of it" he kept repeating but I refused. "I'll die," he said once. "So what", I answered.

I started to be concerned over the possibility that they could really be the vanguard of a larger group. If others showed up I wouldn't be able to control the situation and they would kill me. It was just two a.m. There was such a long wait for the sun to come up, so much time alone with these guys who kept insisting they were part of an army, that I was afraid. I decided to change my weapon, an antique of the sixties, for one they had brought. Carefully I moved to the car and took the new piece. Now I could be sure that every time I pressed the trigger a bullet would be fired.

The wounded man seemed to be fainting. The other two begged me for help, "let us bandage him a bit", but I continued to refuse. "I'm going to die right here", the wounded man cried. "That's your problem", I answered.

I shot up to the sky every so often to call the attention of the coast guard or anyone on the coast to come support me. I would have liked to cure the wounded man, but it was too much of a risk: I wasn't up to it. Sitting on the Lada hood, I kept watch on my prisoners leaning against the truck on their backs, one bleeding and the other two offering me money, a watch, respect for my life when the others showed up, in exchange for their freedom. The hours moved slowly and daylight was slow in arriving. "Lower your pants" I ordered. "One by one, and to the ankles", I added. "You want to kill us", they said. It was the truth. With their pants down they couldn't run while I shot at them. I jumped from the car ready to fire. The wounded man cried noisily; the other two turned their heads timidly. The wounded man cried out again. "You're already half dead", I thought and then saw other lights coming up from the coast.

They were my buddies. Just seeing them I noticed that time began to move at a good pace. Then the soldiers arrived and I handed over the prisoners and I watched them move along the pedraplén in search of the rest of the group. When the sun came up, they told me they were seven, that the rest they caught right away but that the ones I had captured had killed Ovidio. I thought of my friends and understood that if I could save one I would have chosen Ovidio. Maybe not another time but, at least, that night. When I was picking up to go home, I approached the Lada for the last time. I went around it with relief and sadness and I discovered, thanks to that silly and casual wish that, in the back seat, almost behind the wheel, there was a book. I picked it up. *Moby Dick* I read and I couldn't help associating that book with the strange title with the novel Ovidio wanted for his son. Perhaps books aren't to blame, perhaps they are the only ones in the world that are completely blameless, but I couldn't take that book to the son of my friend, the book that belonged to one of his murderers. "I'll get him another copy", I thought. "I don't know where, but I'll get it", I told myself while I dropped it there on the ground.

On October 15, 1994, a group of terrorists of Cuban origin at the service of the Cuban American National Foundation infiltrated the coasts of Caibarién, Villa Clara province and killed the citizen, Arcilio Rodríguez García.

178

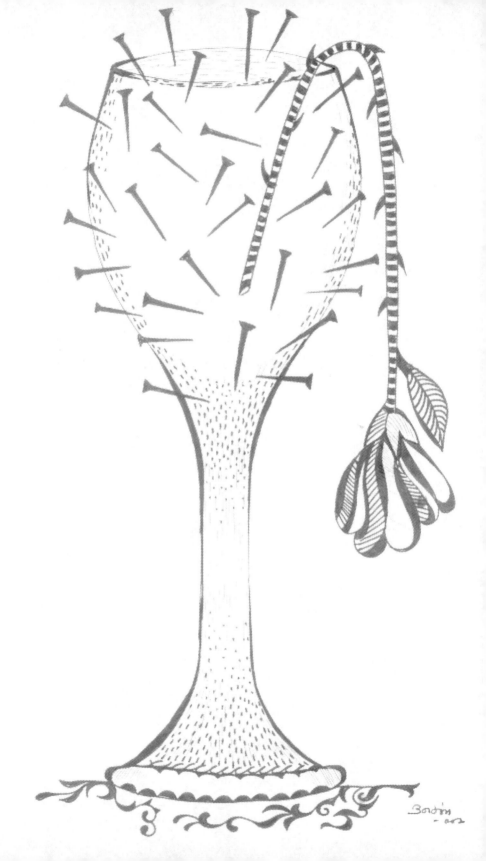

BECAUSE OF A DAMN NOSY SPANISH KID

No man, no. Killing for killing's sake is trivial. I'm not one of those sadistic characters that enjoy the suffering of the rest. I got into the profession when I saw the Rambo films and later Jackal. And there, yes, bud, I discovered that this was my thing. And I got so excited that I started to kill calves, just to practice. And after I did my first jobs, I wanted no other profession […] No then, the business in the circus and the drumming in the Two Shows was just to get myself some rich mommas … […] That's it, just to live well and make a lot of money […] Of course, what I like is to rent planes, jump with parachute and eat well and leave tips and I always thought that when I made a lot of dough I'd go to Las Vegas, in first class, naturally, and get me a couple of high priced white chicks as the Jackal would do. […] Of course, he was paid a nice bundle for each job. […] To me? Well, just a drop. Only thirty thousand pesos for each bomb […] About thirty five hundred dollars […] Well you have to start somewhere […] Let me see if I remember. I bought my mama a music box, some luxury towels for my girl with whom I spent a few days in a five star hotel […] That's the way it was when I returned from my first trip to Cuba. And here I had a good time with some Cuban women who were hand made by God, in hotels with pools and look … […] What? […] Yes, but, you know what gets me most about my work? Well, its excitement, just for the adventure and danger, I would even do it for kicks … […] What's that you say? […] Well, at the beginning, being paid for a hit isn't so easy, it depends where and how things are, because, at times, you have to work in a street full of people and you feel like the whole fucking world is watching you and then you chicken out but later, when you gain confidence and learn to work smoothly, without rushing, everything comes out all right […] No man, because when you start to practice you look for an isolated and dark place and there's no reason to chicken out, its even fun, but when it's a job … […] No, look here, the first time was in Guatemala, after shooting a guy three times, I got on the motorcycle so stressed out that I almost made mincemeat of myself against a truck …[…] Afraid to talk? No, man, even so, I've nothing to lose. The lawyer says that they will probably lower my sentence to thirty years. And Fidel doesn't gain anything by killing me because, nowadays, capital punishment is against human rights. Well … you know that everything is democratic in the United States. And I'm here, great, with my future assured because when this government falls and the Miami people come to run this country, they'll let me out […] And that's what I like, flowers and shit, laws too, yes sir and work for everyone and that decent people find good jobs and that sons of bitches like you, can also make a living working for the narcs or like me, being a hit man, to each according to his capacity but doing what one likes to do in life, do you understand? […] O.K. but I've already explained it to you, dummy …[…] No, what happened was after seeing Rambo and Jackal, all the guys in El Salvador wanted to be like them. You remember the seen where the Jackal takes a watermelon the size of a man's head and bursts it with a shot? I saw it seventeen times … […] If I liked it? And it reached my heart to see how well the Jackal lived and how he dressed and the scarves he tied around his neck and his good manners he has when he eats. And why couldn't I be a gentleman like him? In a democracy, everything is possible. The first thing I did to see if I had cold blood, I practiced … Of course, kill a nobody. I stole a taxi in San Salvador and went to Zacamil when it was dark …[…] No, stupid, I said getting dark. Dark now, who the hell dares to walk around Zacamil? And I stopped at a corner, near the movie theater and the first guy that approaches I put a bullet in his head. […] No man, I first asked about an address and when he approached I thought, you poor son of a bitch, if you only knew…, but what I managed to say, die bastard, your time has come and buuuuum, and seeing his head blown up I felt like the Jackal with the watermelon, all of a professional, do you understand me? It's not that I like to kill. I just wanted to learn how to do things well and be sure I wouldn't be afraid, nor remorse, nor any of the stuff the priests teach. And that is when I knew that that I didn't have to be a Gringo, nor an Englishman, nor a guy like the Jackal, I could also be a good killer. […] The next day when I saw the photo of the guy, a university student who was leaving his girlfriend's house, I didn't feel anything. The color photo in the press showed the blood and brains good and clear; they had splattered a post and the wall of a neighboring house. […] Yes, a few days later I hit a cyclist. I stopped him when he was reaching Santa Tecla, under La Ceiba and I also shot him in the head with a forty five bullet. And when I found out that he was fourteen years old and lived with his mother and that he was the third of five brothers, with no father, I felt that I had done him a favor. And maybe I did the Italian a favor too. […] Yes, the one I killed with the bomb in the Copacabana hotel … […] Do you know the story of the little bird who was dying of the cold and cow dung falls on him? […] Of course, the warmth revived him but at noon the dung dried and got hard and the little bird moved about trying to get it off and a fox seeing it move ate it. And that teaches you that everyone who shits wants to fuck you; and that not everyone who wants to get the shit off you wants to save you and the one who is covered in shit, cannot go about moving much. […] You laugh? Look, that is the same thing that happened to the Italian because, you tell me, let's see? What was that bastard Italian doing in a hotel so far from home? If he wanted to do the tourist bit why didn't he stay in Italy that they say is so pretty and so many people go? Why did he have to move about so much? And as *maistro* Posada Carriles would say, that Italian was in the wrong place at the wrong moment. I didn't tell him to go there. *Nothing personal, you understand?* […] And, as I was saying, I certainly did a favor to the bastard on the bike because I later found at that he had just stolen it and he was going around crazy because his mama had become a prostitute and he surely got it from his older brothers and did it to his younger ones. What's the life of a bum like this worth? That is why I'm telling you that I am not sentimental, nor do I have any old hang ups, nor do I want to get my own

183

back for anything when I was a kid. I hold no resentment against anyone; but, also, I don't feel for anyone what they call affection. And, I think that life is like a jungle. The big animals eat the little ones. That's how God fixed this puzzle of life and that is why you have to grab on to life as it comes. […] Later? Well, later when I was sure that I could be like the Jackal I became a hit man. […] Yup, for the narcs. And I was always straight and serious in my work and one day *maistro* Posada Carriles sent for me…[…] What's that you say? […] No, that's too long a story. […] Of course they trained me well […] No, I made no mistake. […] Well it was just bad luck because that day I had placed the first two bombs with no problems, the first in the hotel Copacabana, where the Italian died and the second in the Chateau Miramar and when I was going to place the third in the Triton hotel, a thirteen or fourteen year old Spanish kid got in the way …[…] Well, a seer kid, son of seven thousand botches…Yes a Spanish kid this size touristing with his family, can you believe it, he guessed what I was going to do…[…] Don't ask me how. I didn't have a sign on my forehead saying I was going to place a bomb. […] Well, it's how I'm telling you, no more than fourteen years old he was sitting over there and when he saw me, he stood up and fixed his eyes on me and if you could see how meanly he was looking at me, as if he guessed what I was going to do, and you won't believe it but it was such a weird look as if he had seen the devil, that he even made me nervous but, what the hell, since I was sure that the kid couldn't know what I was going to do I walked past and, like always, I locked myself in the bathroom, armed my trinket, put its *timing* for twelve thirty and went to sit in the lobby in the place I had chosen but there was that damned kid again who wouldn't take his eyes off me and he was with a girl of about twenty who I later learned was his older sister and when it was twelve twenty I went to sit behind them, on a sofa against the wall, but not completely, and there, behind the sofa I was going to leave the bag…[…] Yes, a plastic bag of the Duty Free Shop where I had placed the activated bomb set for twelve thirty two and then, so as not to call attention, I start looking at photos that I had taken in the streets of Havana, and, can you believe it? The son of a gun turns around and continues to spy on me. And there I was, controlling the hour, twelve twenty three and twenty five and the damn kid there, in his seat with his eyes boring on me and I am angry now, wanting him to blow up in little pieces…[…] Well, it would be his fault for being a busybody and when

184

it was twelve twenty six, at a moment the kid turns to talk to his sister and stops looking at me for a moment, I let the bomb drop to the floor behind the sofa back and I run quickly to the door and grab a taxi right there and take off for La Bodeguita del Medio where I was going to place the fourth bomb and then I hear buuuuum at twelve twenty nine in the Copa and at twelve thirty another buuuuum, the bomb in the Chateau and at thirty two buuuuum, the one I had just left in the Triton and I imaging the son of a bitch kid flying through the air and I act stupid and ask the taxi driver about the explosions and the SOB says their dynamiting rocks near by to build a new hotel and when we reach a light, a policeman with a walky-talky makes signs to the cab driver to pull up and the son of a bitch bends down to look inside…[…] Yes, well like in the movies and he looks at me with a serious face and me, I'm shitting, because imagine, I had with me the bomb I was going to place in La Bodeguita del Medio this afternoon and if the cop decides to search me …[…] Oh yes, what happened with the kid. What I learned later was that when he saw me leave he pulled on the sister's sleeve telling her that I had placed a bomb and making a racket and shouting to her to get out of there and, all of a sudden buuuuum, the explosion and when Intelligence officers arrived they interrogated the kid and I think that he made a spoken picture that was like a photograph, yes, in colors and the kid got me right and that same afternoon I was arrested and they brought the damn dogs and they started barking the moment they smelled me, it looked like they wanted to eat me …[…] Yes, as if they were furious with me…[…] But if that kid had not been so nosy they would never have found me…[…] No no, that same afternoon, I placed my last bomb in La Bodeguita with no trouble at all and when I left I breathed deeply. I had fulfilled my mission and the next morning I was going to leave the country. I had my return ticket with the Ok and all, in Mexicana de Aviación. But when I arrived at the hotel the police were there waiting for me. In truth I followed to a tee what my instructor told me and made no mistake. None. It was all the fault of bitchy bad luck and the damned Spanish kid.

Havana, August 2002

On July 12, 1997, a Salvadoran mercenary, hired by the terrorist of Cuban origin, Luis Posada Carriles at the service of the Cuban American National Foundation, placed four bombs in four tourist installations in Havana before being captured.

THE CHILD AND THE WOMAN COP

The world awaits the year 2000. There is a friendly universal controversy over whether it is the beginning of a new century and new millennium or if these events should be celebrated twelve months later considering 2001 the beginning of the new century.

Paris already has more lights than ever lit. That night the City of Light will become day at noon; it is 31 December, 1999. In Times Square, New York, an impressive multitude, from many parts of the world, await the 21st century. The neon lights with images in movement compete in beauty and some people hold a bunch of red grapes: it is the most splendid tourism that any person can image. The electronic development fascinates. In the homes people await the sound of the twelve gongs, depending on the hemisphere. Early during the day television channels begin to broadcast details of the millions of people watching giant screens placed in the most centric places of capitals and emblematic cities. Some are drinking champagne in trips from one continent to another at a height of thousands of feet and are able to welcome the New Year in several countries and several times in 24 hours. China will have two celebrations; one on that day and another for the New

Lunar Year later on. Expectations of joy will differ and will be noisy; the music and dances different.

Not many people in the history of humanity have the opportunity of living in two centuries and much less, to pass from one millennium to another, to live in the future at least for a few hours; even the poor and unfortunate await the year 2000, filled with hope. For older cultures it will be the year 6000 or, who knows, but for us it is the second millennium of a Christian era. And, when was Christ born? It doesn't matter. With his birth, our world entered a new era and it was reason enough to have a great celebration.

However, in a pearly island or thorn driven into the sea separating two American territories, things are different. Happiness, when it exists, is enjoyed with modesty, in intimacy. Families get together the night before, like any New Year. But there is a common sorrow that withers happiness. The day after 31 December, 1999, the newspapers will simply typeset the new date on the front page: "Year 2000" to be followed by events that concern and sadden us.

It just so happens that the television is showing the confused look of a kidnapped child who lives through terror a few miles from the coast. With the child victim among Miami "wolves there was no reason to celebrate the New Year. The child has been seen looking out from a door that he himself closes, dressed in clothing that typify his prison. He must have come upon the face of his mother in a grotesque poster– in infamous torture – who he lost at sea. That and his surroundings confuse him since the day of being rescued from the sea in a disorderly immigration that the terrorist who "took him in" – "male and female wolves" – constantly encourage. He doesn't know this; he is innocent although imprisoned.

The people have also seen him, holding on to a bit of joy while he innocently plays in his detention center and suddenly hears an airplane. He looks up and shouts: *I want to be taken back to Cuba.* The metal bird is deaf and dumb and so continues on its way. His eyes, for the first time with a happy look follow the plane until it disappears from view. His candid slip will cost a punishment to the captive. They will pinch him: his terrorist kidnappers, trained to destroy the mind of a child, who do not stop threatening him. They are following to a "t", like perfect employees, the macabre plan to destroy his happy memories while making him a "child merchandize" which can fully fill their pockets.

188

Then we have seen that there is sufficient reason in the pearly Island and the thorny island of the neighbor that harbors crows to prevent joining the world in the universal celebration of the year 2000, the beginning of the Third Millennium.

He, the child, must remember little or not at all, his odyssey in the Florida Straits.

Those who do remember and will never be able to forget for the rest of their lives, like a punishment, are the only two survivors of the tragedy in the sea – that repeats itself in different forms many times – the two are hidden in the shadows and it seems have fled Miami, they hide. When the child was found by two fishermen he was asleep in inner tube. The sea at night must have been a terrible experience that the fragile body of the boy left him exhausted. He either fell asleep or had fainted.

They say he never spoke of the tragedy at sea he simply says *what happened to me* and no more.

A puppy is his cute companion on land; he talks with the puppy. Since these relatives acting like prison wardens film their "merchandize" that has given them so much profit, the Island has seen his communion with the little dog, the only one that doesn't harm the "golden" prisoner. According to the psychologists, a complicity of silence was established between the puppy and the child. The silence would bring him peace after having to walk with the terrorist Mafiosi – J.M.S., "king" of the Mafia as chauffer – in luxury cars sounding their horns, at times escorted by fire trucks open the way for the caravan that carries him like a trophy, announcing his passing, being filmed at all times, in every place, stealing his innocence.

Those days, when we saw him on television, the kidnapped boy had no light in his face. In fact, the only communication of love up to then was when the plane flew overhead when he asked for his return to Cuba.

There, in his cruel confinement he understood, instinctively, that he was an object for interested exhibition: *money is money*.

One day they asked him what had happened he simply said: "My mother died" and no more although he did not know what death was. The promoters of death through the Law of Cuban Adjustment – that is the name of death at sea, the greater probability of illegal immigration – continued to take advantage of his charisma, of his infant beauty, of his innocence. In the meantime, a battle of intelligence was flaring up, a war of ideas and emotions in support of the return of the child to his father.

The international press compares his case to the kidnapping of the Lindbergh baby. The kidnapping of the aviator's child shook the United States and the world half a century ago. And the people of that country could have linked that action with the kidnapping of the "child rafter" – although for different reasons – or they rejected the terror inflicted upon the innocent boy. Anything could happen, but what is true and real is that once the truth of the kidnapping came out and the denial of Parental Rights of his father, Elian – who was the child imprisoned by the terrorist – had another bond, another ally in his defense, that gave happiness to his heart, in addition to the metal bird that crossed the sky. That is why, when he was with his father in Wye plantation, in the north, far from the Island, even the guards of the State of the Union who protected him from the kidnappers taught the child to ride a bicycle and played hide and seek with him. Six feet tall men, of hardened muscles, appropriate for the task, played under equal conditions with Elian although technically it was the human manner of respecting his childish games and have him in sight, protected in the plantation where the innocent child was waiting for the court to return him to his father, his family and his country.

By then his mind had registered and kept a kind voice of a person unknown to him, and will never forget when he puts together the pieces of the puzzle of those days, the voice of the Woman Cop – who in moments of great hopes, violence and fear, when he was being taken from the kidnappers, at D time, the rescue, she carried him and holding him close to his breast kept repeating with tenderness: *Be calm, we are going to see your father. Don't cry; don't cry that we are going to see your father. We are going to see your papa, your papa... you're going to see your papa; I'm taking you to your papa. Now you are going to see your papa.*

September 19, 2002

On Monday of November 22, 1999, fourteen illegal emigrants, in a frail boat capsized off the coasts of Florida and a 5 year old boy, Elian Gonzalez was discovered floating on an inner tube close to the Miami coast. For seven months he was kept against the will of his father by kidnappers manipulated by the Cuban American National Foundation. After a legal process that reached the US Supreme Court and with the support of 80 percent of the US population the child was permitted to return to his father and Cuba.

ricardo alarcón de quesada

EPILOGUE The texts that make up this book, contrary to the explanations that tend to accompany fiction films, all refer directly to real persons or events. Its reading gives us the chance to relive hours of suffering and pain that are an inseparable part of the personal life of each one of us.

Gerardo Hernández, Ramón Labañino, Fernando González, Antonio Guerrero and René González were not born yet or were barely beginning to live when Washington sponsored terrorism, left death and destruction in their people, They are part of a generation of Cubans that have had to bear, day and night, during their entire life, the most ruthless, sinister and pro-longed war.

There are many reasons for the solidarity in favor of these heroes in the face of the terrible injustice they and their families suffer. However, there is one supreme reason to make the effort to free them in a real national battle because it refers, literally, to the right to life of an entire people.

The case of our five compatriots is irrefutable proof that this war – and specially its most appalling manifestation, terrorism – not only continues today but also intends to maintain it forever and threatens Cubans not yet born.

Their arbitrary arrest on September 12, 1998; the brutal jail conditions to which they were submitted; the numerous manipulations and violations of legal procedures; the verdicts, sentences; cruel treatment they still suffer, and the almost complete silence of the great "information" mass media; this sordid process has only one explanation: The United States will continue to promote terrorism against Cuba and, for this reason, it punishes with irrational cruelty those who dared to confront the terrorists and they make sure that the so-called "free" press – or "disciplined" press, as Chomsky likes to call it – does not report anything.

Everything, however, is well documented.

Throughout the period that preceded the public hearing in the Miami court trying the case, the District Attorney of South Florida (the government) took care to protect the terrorist groups that attack Cuba from its territory: I declare the subject of terrorism totally excluded in these hearings, that members of these groups not be called to testify and that if they must do so, their testimonies be covered by the Fifth Amendment (meaning that they reveal nothing). All these decisions are in writing in official documents of the government. The acknowledgment of crimes by some of the terrorists appear in the court records as also the irrefutable proof of these actions presented by the defense attorneys of our compatriots.

As if this insolence were not enough, at the time of sentencing, both the government and court openly decreed that the purpose of the "trial" was to protect these terrorist groups. The government formally requesting, in a written demand and, in addition, imposing the maximum sentence against the five heroes, included incapacitation to carry out any actions against the terrorists once they recover their freedom. The judge, accepting the request, unbelievably added these words to the sentence: "As a special condition to granting supervised freedom the accused are forbidden to meet with or visit places that are known meeting places of terrorists, of members of organizations that promote violence or figures of organized crime."

At first, they were accused of conspiring to commit espionage. They were described as spies by the authorities and all the Miami press that unwaveringly condemned them from the very first day they were arrested. Nevertheless, no proof was ever presented, no document or secret material that they had allegedly obtained, no witness to testify that they had tried to get confidential information. Quite the contrary. There were witnesses of great authority – generals, admirals, US security agencies – who declared under oath that none of the accused had done any of these things. They had not spied, there was no attempt to spy nor were they ordered to spy.

An additional charge was leveled against Gerardo Hernández, even more false, absurd and infamous: conspiring to kill with premeditation. He was presented as being responsible for the death of those who lost their lives on February 24, 1996, in an incident that occurred when the Cuban air force, exercising its legitimate national sovereignty, shot down two planes. These were from a Miami based terrorist group and were downed after violating Cuban air space for purposes of provocation, subversion and to carry out sabotages.

Aside from the fact that this unfortunate event was not a case of murder and that the incident was the result of the aggressive policy of the United States against Cuba and its right and obligation to defend itself, Gerardo had absolutely nothing to do with the events.

The accusation against Gerardo clearly demonstrates the false motive of this case and the absolute absence of ethics of the United States authorities. They added this accusation in May of 1999, six months after the five Cubans were imprisoned – in solitary confinement for the entire period – after being formally accused of other charges. They did so after the Miami press revealed meetings of the district attorney's office with elements of the anti–Cuban terrorist Mafia where these individuals openly requested the addition of this completely false charge.

This irresponsible slander turned to dust during the court sessions. Numerous evidence was presented on the violations of Cuban air space, including the violation that fateful day, and on the activities and terrorist plans promoted by these groups and referring to the guilty conduct of the United States government that even knew beforehand of the provocation planned for that date. Obviously, against Gerardo there was no proof, no witness, nothing that linked him with the events.

On May 25, 2001, when the trial concluded, the United States government took an unprecedented step. It requested that the Appeals Court modify its own accusation that "in view of the proof presented in the trial" it faced "an insurmountable obstacle ... and that would probably lead to the failure of the accusation of the charges". In other words, they were forced to acknowledge what was already known: that they never had any proof, because it was impossible to have them, that Gerardo had not killed anyone and much less with premeditation. The authorities always knew that they would be unable to prove a slander that was totally an invention. When they introduced the charge in the initial stage of the process they simply wanted to satisfy the desire for revenge of the terrorist Mafia and give them an element that would poison, even more, the environment to completely prevent a trial with even an appearance of normalcy.

The Appellate Court did not accept the district attorney's request and, as a result, the jury had to decide if Gerardo was guilty or innocent of the charge made against him two years before.

Then something unbelievable occurred that could only happen in a Miami court: without doubts, without any doubt or request for clarification, with untold speed, the jury declared Gerardo guilty of first-degree murder. He was found guilty of something that not even the prosecution was now accusing him of.

The conduct of the jury – as that of the judge and the prosecution – the obvious was confirmed: in Miami, it is impossible to objectively try the Cuban Revolution and its representatives. How can this be ignored since there bombs have exploded and those who wanted to hear Rosita Fornés or the Van Van were threatened; if there, in full view and with nazi savagery a painting by Mendive was destroyed; if there, Elian Gonzalez was kidnapped for four months against what the government and the courts had ruled or the laws and human decency demanded; if the Latin Grammys awards had to be moved, not once but twice, from Miami fearing the safety and physical integrity of the artists and participants.

That was the key question to solve the very moment our five compatriots were submitted to a trial and the defense lawyers demanded from the beginning. They requested that their defendants be granted their Constitutional rights, contemplated in the laws and unalterable US tradition, to be tried in another place with an impartial jury. The prosecution stubbornly refused. It said that Miami is not what everyone says Miami is. It unblushingly affirmed that an impartial trial was possible there against the five Cuban patriots, only guilty of acting against the interest of the terrorist Mafia that controls that city. In spite of the insistence of the accused and their lawyers, court appointed lawyers who had complained to the court of the pressure to which they and their family were submitted, the judge sided with the position of the government and denied the five their basic rights. The trial had to be held in

196

Miami. Announcing her decision, the judge made a declaration on March 16, 2000, that was so surprising and revealing: "This trial will be more interesting than any television program."

On November 12, 2002, Leonard Weinglass, lawyer for Antonio Guerrero and backed by the other defense lawyers, requested the Miami court to reject the previous view and hold a new trial outside the city.

The main reason supporting this motion is the fraudulent conduct of the prosecution and the judge in the management of the original demand of the defense that had requested, for several times, since January of 2000 that the trial be held outside Miami.

The district attorney of Florida strongly opposed a change of venue for the trial of the five. However, one year later, on June 25, 2002, the same office regarding a civil suit (Ramírez vs. Ashcroft), the accused was granted a change of venue using the same principle and right that it had rejected previously in the case against the five.

The legal precedent in both cases was the same: Pamplin vs. Mason of 1968. When used for Antonio Guerrero the prosecution argued that it was inapplicable in his case because Miami–Dade is an "urban center" that is "extremely varied", "politically non–monolithic" and with a "great diversity" and, therefore, she considered that a fair and impartial trial free from "external influence" was possible. When she was the accused, the same prosecution noted that Miami–Dade is a community with deep–rooted sentiments and deep prejudices regarding Cuba where a fair and impartial trial was "virtually impossible".

The judge, for her part, committed several violations that contributed to deprive the accused of their most elemental rights that consisted in the manner in which the testimony of professor Morán was treated, an expert hired by the court at the request of the defense; it violated the *ex parte* nature of the request by which the request wrongfully communicated to the prosecution, concealed negative antecedents that existed in its relations with this expert, she delayed and manipulated payment for his services, rejected his results with superficial and false arguments and manipulated the data and denied the request for a change of venue basing the criteria on her decision that contradicted federal law.

The motion presented before the Miami court demanding a new trial, analyses in depth and with legal rigor of the violations of the prosecution and

197

the judge, has several annexes with documents and sworn declarations that amply proves the right of this petition and the need of a new trial for the five Cuban patriots, outside Miami, in view of the new evidence uncovered and in the interest of justice.

Gerardo Hernández, Ramón Labañino, Antonio Guerrero, Fernando González and René González, Heroes of the Republic of Cuba, are also heroes of culture. They are five intellectuals who think and create in the most hostile and difficult conditions. Five intellectuals jailed for their ideas and ideals, for having fought – without weapons, without the use of violence – against terrorists who act with impunity, using in that battle only their intelligence, talent and self–sacrifice, without any weapons but convictions and an admirable spirit of sacrifice.

They continue to fight in their unfair and harsh incarceration. They do not stop writing or drawing. They communicate with thousands of persons around the world in verse and in prose. The message they send – their main sustenance that encourages the international movement for their freedom – is an invaluable contribution to culture. It confirms that nothing can imprison a free and creative spirit

January 2, 2003.

ricardo alarcón de quesada

"The sun of justice shall rise,
bearing salvation on its wings"
(Malaquías, 4, 2)

The Cuban Five in Atlanta: A Long March Towards Justice

On 9th August last, 28 months after the defendants had filed their arguments, the 11th Circuit Court of Appeals in Atlanta finally handed down its verdict reversing the unjust convictions imposed over four years ago by a Miami Court on five young Cuban anti-terrorism fighters. The decision of the Atlanta Court was in no way a precipitated one. The process enabling the defendants to exercise their right of appeal was long, complex and hazardous. They had to face a whole series of obstacles that breached principles and rules of both American and international law, which forced them to a defense in conditions that defy imagination. It seemed their case would never actually reach the superior court for its necessary review. Then, the judges in Atlanta in order to do justice dedicated to the case four times the period used by the shameful farce in Miami[1].

[1] District Court No. 98-00721-CR-JAL. The document issued by the Atlanta Court is 93 pages long. The court's decision to reverse the convictions of the Miami Court and annul the previous "trial" was based on Miami's denial of the various requests to have the trial moved to another venue. In arriving at its decision, Atlanta found it necessary to "review the totality of the circumstances surrounding the trial", including the "evidence" submitted and other

199

The Atlanta decision has a truly historical significance.

To understand it, it is necessary to put it in context and to go over - albeit briefly - the events leading up to it.

On September 12th, 1998, the FBI arrested Gerardo Hernández, Ramón Labañino, Antonio Guerrero, Fernando González and René González. They were accused of being unregistered agents of the Cuban government, whose mission was to infiltrate - with the aim of revealing their criminal plans - the terrorist groups that operate with impunity out of Miami. None of the men had criminal records; none had ever been accused of breaking any law or infringing any rule or regulation. They were unarmed and had never been involved in acts of violence or disturbances of any kind. They were none-theless denied the possibility of applying for a release on bail.

On the contrary, from the very day of their arrest, they were put in soli-tary confinement - locked up in the infamous "hole", where they remained for a continuous period of 17 months. They were subjected to an entirely illegal punishment regime, restricted by US law to dangerous criminals who commit acts of violence inside the prison, and to a maximum of 60 days. They were prevented from mounting their defence while a massive, ruthless press campaign was unleashed in Miami with the participation of the pros-ecution, the FBI officials and the local authorities, portraying them as dan-gerous enemies guilty of the worst crimes, including the attempt "to destroy the United States"[2]. Condemned in advance without trial or possibility of defence, they were subjected to a barrage of slander and threats.

But that was not enough for their accusers. To make quite sure that justice could not prevail, the government (with the agreement of the Miami

---

aspects of the earlier proceedings. The length of the document and the exhaustiveness of its coverage are unusual, as were the time taken to produce it and the complete unanimity of the three judges concerned. While what took place in Miami was a charade that shames the American legal system, Atlanta produced an example of professional ethics and rigour that goes beyond the bounds of the normal appeals process, to demonstrate the innocence of the five accused and expose the colossal injustice to which they fell victim.

[2] The employment of this argument, obviously false and aimed at pressuring the jury and encouraging and exploiting the hostility and prejudices of the Miami community against the accused, was one of the examples cited by the Atlanta judges to demonstrate the fraudulent conduct of the South Florida District Attorney's office. The then DA, Guy Lewis (now retired) published an article in the Miami Herald on August 18th repeating the same foolish slander: he still insists that the five men "had vowed to destroy the United States".

Court) classified as secret the alleged "evidence", much of which belonged to the defendants themselves and included family photographs, personal correspondence and recipes. The defendants and their attorneys were thus denied access to the material, while the government was able to arbitrarily use and manipulate it. The defence is still now awaiting permission to view this "evidence". It has vainly claimed it time and again before the Miami Court and appealed in this connection to the Atlanta Court; it has still received no reply.

These were the circumstances in which the "trial" opened, on November 27th, 2000. 26 months had gone by since the day of the five men's arrest. And let us not forget that they spent 17 of those 26 months buried in the "hole".

The Miami judicial farce ended in June 2001 when a submissive, frightened jury, which had announced in advance the date and precise hour at which it would deliver its verdicts, found them guilty on all 26 counts, after deliberations lasting just a few hours and without asking a single question or expressing the slightest doubt. To cap it all, it found Gerardo Hernández guilty of something - the infamous Charge 3, first-degree murder - that the prosecution itself, in the knowledge that it could not be proved, had applied to withdraw it.[3]

Surprisingly, having arrived so quickly and easily at the desired verdict, the judge took six months to pronounce the sentences. She took as long as the "trial" itself. Why? Was she about to change or amend in some way the conduct of the jury? Was she trying to distance herself at least to some extent from the prosecution's request?

Nothing of the sort. The disproportionate sentences were exactly those the government had proposed. Was it necessary to delay half a year to respond? Why the long wait?

---

[3] In its "emergency petition for writ of prohibition" to the Court of Appeals on May 25, 2001, the U.S. Attorney's Office recognized that "in light of the evidence presented in this trial, this presents an insurmountable hurdle for the United States in this case, and will likely result in the failure of the prosecution on this count" (page 21) since it "imposes an insurmountable barrier to this prosecution" (page 27). The government was afraid of the fact that "it is highly probable that the jury will request further elaboration on this issue" (pages 20 - 21). (Emergency Petition for Writ of Prohibition). Nevertheless, although the court rejected the Government's petition, nothing alike happen. Without any question, without hesitation, all the jurors declared Gerardo guilty in the first degree of the alleged crime.

At the end of the trial, the judge announced that she would proceed to sentence in September. While she took vacation, the five were returned to solitary confinement. This time, they remained in the "hole" for 48 days, and got out only after several efforts by their attorneys. This further arbitrary treatment had a clear purpose: to make preparation of their statements - their only opportunity to address the court - as difficult as possible. When the time came, instead of apologizing or seeking clemency, as convicted prisoners generally do, the five vigorously condemned the farcical proceedings and exposed the terrorists and the Government that supports and protects them.

But something else happened in September 2001. The odious crime committed on the 11th had shaken American society and the whole world; the judge decided to postpone the sentencing sessions. It was an unusual deferral: three months. It was not mourning of or homage to the victims of that atrocity which caused the delay. Rather, it was quite the opposite.

Her reasons were utterly different. What she and the government were proposing to do was, among other things, a gross affront to the victims of that fateful day. They needed to separate the two events by as large an interval as possible, and gain enough time to ensure maximum impunity, relying on the customary cooperation of the information-suppressing mass media.

The government was going to bring to a climax a manoeuvre designed to support and protect the terrorists with whom the Bush family has close and longstanding links, and to whom the current tenant of the White House had promised reward in kind for the scandalous fraud by which he obtained the presidency in 2000.

That was why, after seeking maximum sentences, the prosecution shamelessly introduced in court proceedings its immoral and illegal theory of "incapacitation": in addition to the exorbitant sentences imposed on the accused, they were to be subjected to very specific restrictions after their release, such that they could never again attempt any action against these murderers who are close friends of the Bush family and behave as if they owned Miami, from where they organize and openly vaunt their misdeeds against the Cuban people.

They could never again be free men. Beyond the years in prison, which included four life sentences, they were to suffer a special regime, a sort of unusual apartheid designed to protect the terrorists. Places were defined which they could not go near, locations they could not visit, streets they would be forbidden to walk in.

The agency tasked with enforcing these spurious, unconstitutional prohibitions would be the FBI. The same FBI that pursued them, mistreated them and fabricated the infamous accusation against them. The same FBI, incidentally, under whose nose most of the terrorists who attacked the American people on September 11th lived, freely moved about and were trained in the use of aircrafts as monstrous weapons.

The judge naturally welcomed the government's request and in the sentences pronounced on René González (15 years imprisonment) and Antonio Guerrero (life, plus ten years), both US citizens by birth, expressed the restrictions in the following terms: "As a further special condition of supervised release the defendant is prohibited from associating with or visiting specific places where individuals or groups such as terrorists, members of organizations advocating violence, and organized crime figures are known to be or frequent". [4]

The defence attorneys immediately notified their intention to appeal to the relevant superior court. But, again, the long wait.

authorities that were so tardy when it came to sending the documents to the principal city of a neighbouring state, which is also one of the US's main centres of communication, lost no time in dispersing the five men to the remotest corners of American territory. Each in a different prison, in five different states, as far separated as possible from one another, from their attorneys and from their relatives.

Their families reside in Cuba and require American visas to visit them, visas that only have been granted after annoying and slow procedures.

---

[4] Transcript of Sentencing Hearing before the Honorable Joan A. Lenard on 14th December 2001 (pp. 45-46). In the same session, the judge herself had recognized that "the terrorist acts committed by others could not excuse the wrongful and illegal conduct of the defendant and the other accused" (p. 43). In other words, the Miami-based anti-Cuba terrorists are protected by the federal government and the judges who punish - with four life sentences over 75 years' imprisonment and the unusual prohibition mentioned above - those who fight terrorism. So that they should never again fall into such "wrongful and illegal" conduct, Miami invented "incapacitation", which it unveiled three months after the atrocity of 11th September 2001, when Bush was already attacking Afghanistan, was preparing to attack Iraq and was declaring an alleged war on terrorism to be waged everywhere - except Miami, of course.

Unlike any other inmate, that elemental right has been denied to the Five: for three of them the visits have not been weekly, but one in a year, and the visas of Adriana Pérez, Gerardo's wife and Olga Salanueva, René's wife, have been systematically denied. Consequently, Ivette, Olga and René's daughter, could not visit her father either.

These were the conditions under which they were to prepare their appeals. All, naturally, in a foreign language. Without access to the "evidence", without the possibility of consulting each other, while communication with their attorneys was extremely limited. And subject to the severest prison regime under which, among other things, they were required to work to pay with their wages for the rigged trial they had undergone.

But, as the Bible says, "Our eyes can never see enough to be satisfied; our ears can never hear enough".

While the five defendants were immersed in this difficult, complex task, under the most hostile conditions vindictively imposed by the federal authorities, the latter's thirst for revenge and desire to obstruct justice were still not satisfied.

For such purposes, there was the "hole", and within that, the "box". And that is where they were confined from February 28th until March 31st, 2003. Each of them, in their five prisons, in the decisive month for their appeals, again in solitary confinement without any contact with the outside world. Moreover, they were now denied any communication with their attorneys, even by telephone or letter, while all writing materials were confiscated - not a sheet of paper or a stub of pencil. One was left without clothes, in the middle of winter, and subjected to physical torture (noises, lights and shouting flooding the "box" twenty-four hours a day).

This time there was not even an attempt to disguise the government's purpose. The men were denied access to their legal documents and their attorneys were not allowed to communicate with their clients. These measures were controlled directly by the South Florida District Attorney's office. It was only international denounce and the tireless efforts of the defence attorneys that forced the authorities to "ease" these measures: Leonard Weinglass, Antonio Guerrero's attorney, was able to visit his client, but under such appalling conditions that he was barely able to verify the gross violations of the right to a defence. Weinglass denounced the situation before the Court of Appeals and requested more time for submitting Antonio's arguments which, because of the situation described, he had been unable to complete. In granting this request, Atlanta acknowledged that these measures had seriously infringed the rights of the accused and their defence attorneys.[5]

In outline, that was the long path travelled by the five men, to reach Atlanta. Getting there was a truly heroic deed.

What came afterwards were another two years of waiting. The three judges took that time to assess the appeal arguments of both sides, study the trial records and all the other material relating to the Miami farce, review the relevant legislation, hold a hearing (on March 10th, 2004) which exposed the shaky foundations of the government's arguments, seek additional information from prosecuting and defence lawyers, working towards their final conclusion revoking convictions and annulling the Miami "trial".

Their decision was announced on August 9th, 2005, but the five men are still being held in the same maximum-security prisons. They are locked up with people presumably convicted of various crimes, while they themselves

[5] Weinglass was able to gain permission to visit Gerardo Hernández on March 16th, and he described his visit in this way:

"Gerardo is being most severely punished in his prison, confined in what is known as "the Box"-a hole within the "Hole".

He is confined in a very small cell barely three paces wide, with no windows and only a slot in the metal door through which food is passed. His clothes were taken from him and he is allowed to wear only underpants and a T-shirt, but no shoes.

He cannot tell if it is day or night. His is the only cell where the lights are on 24 hours a day and the incessant cries of other prisoners, many of whom suffer from mental health problems, prevent him from sleeping.

He is allowed no printed material, nothing to read. Signs saying that no one is to have contact with him are posted outside his cell. He is the only prisoner kept in this kind of solitary confinement who is not allowed to use the telephone to date he has received nothing - not even correspondence from his attorneys"

Two days later he outlined in this way his meeting with Antonio:

"He showed up at the visit in leg irons and handcuffed. They were removed during the visit. The corridors were cleared when moving him. The visiting facility was abysmal. It was a very small cubby with a thick glass between us and a telephone which we had to use to communicate. The space was so small that my associate counsel and I could not fit in it together. He had to stand behind me and share the one phone on our end. Antonio was locked in on his side and we, the attorneys, were also locked in on our side! There was no slot for passing documents and we were invited to give them to the guards who would bring them around the back to Antonio. I did this with one document and then decided to abandon this and hold the papers up to the glass. It was very awkward. The visiting conditions were much worse than those I experienced with Mumia Abu Jamal on death row. We protested these conditions but they refused to bring the warden down for a meeting or any other ranking official"

are different from the rest of the inmates, being the only ones now without any conviction.

It is of no consequence to the US government that the Atlanta Court of Appeals has pronounced them free men against whom no legal sanction now remains. It was unmoved also in May of this year when a working group on arbitrary detention set up by the UN Human Rights Commission declared the incarceration of the five men since September 1998 arbitrary and illegal.

Two weeks have passed, out of the three the law allows the government, to request the Atlanta Court to revoke its finding. So far, Washington has not said whether it intends to do so. Indeed, it has just asked the Court for another month to decide whether to make the request.

Meanwhile, the five men remain isolated in five prisons for convicted criminals. They are suffering all the rigours of that situation, despite their false culpability had already been annulled by three honorable judges.

Now they are five kidnap victims of an administration that rides roughshod over the law everywhere. Not just in Abu Grahib and Guantánamo. Within US territory as well.

What is to be done? The time has come to shout it from the rooftops. To go on demanding their immediate release until it happens, unconditionally. Freedom now for the Cuban Five. Nothing more. Nothing less.

August, 2005

THE AUTHORS

Roberto Fernández Retamar
(Havana, 1930). He studied in the Universities of Havana (where he is an honorary professor), Paris and London. He has offered courses and conferences in many others in America, Europe and Japan and in many, he was awarded an Honoris Causa Doctorate. He is the president of the Casa de las Americas since 1986. He has published many books of poetry from *Elegía como un himno* (1950) to *Aquí* (Madrid, 2000) as well as studies and essays from *La poesía contemporánea en Cuba, 1927-1953* (1954) to *Concierto para la mano izquierda* (2001). Included among the awards he has received the following can be mentioned: the Félix Varela Order, 1981 and the National Prize for Literature, 1989; the Latin American Rubén Darío Poetry Award, 1980, in Nicaragua; the Official Medal of the Order of Arts and Literature, 1994, in France; the Feronia Prize, 2001, in Italy and is a Puterbaugh Fellow, 2002, in the United States.

Juan V. Rodríguez Bonachea (Havana, 1957). Painter and professor. He has had more than one hundred personal and collective exhibitions. He has illustrated books for children for young people and for adults. He has murals in different provinces in the country. Part of his work is in private collections in Spain, France, United States and Switzerland. In 1988, he received the Third Prize in the NOMA Contest in Tokyo; in 1990, the Third Prize for the National Salon of Illustration, Havana, and in 1992, he received a Mention for Graphic Arts from the Gráfico *Revista Plural,* Mexico City, among others.

Eduardo Heras León (Havana, 1940). Professor, narrator, journalist, literary and dance critic, editor. Among his books published there are: *La guerra tuvo seis nombres* (David Award, for short stories, 1968); *Los pasos en la hierba* (Mention, Casa de las Américas Contest, for short stories, 1970); *Acero* (short story, 1977); *A fuego limpio* (short story, 1981); *Cuestión de principio* (UNEAC National Award, short stories, 1983 and the Critic Prize, 1986); *La nueva guerra* (short story,1990), and *La noche del capitán* (short story, 1995). In 1990, he received the National Culture Distinction.

THE CIGARETTE CASE /19

Waldo Leyva (Las Villas, 1943). Poet, narrator and journalists. Included among his publications are: *De la ciudad y sus héroes* (Poetry Prize, 1976); *Angola desde aquí* (testimony, 1985); *Memoria del porvenir* (poetry, 1999), and *La distancia y el tiempo* (poetry anthology, 2002) and a CD of his poetry musicalized *Definitivamente jueves* (EGREM, 2000).

Julio Girona (Manzanillo, 1914-Havana, 2002). Painter, sculptor and professor. He had about eighty personal and collective experiences. During the Spanish Civil War he drew for several anti-fascist newspapers. In the fifties and sixties took part in the abstract-expressionist movement in New York A large part of his work is in collections such as in the Cuban National Museum of Fine Arts, Union Carbide, Museums of Trenton and Newark in the United States and Dortmund University and Fritz Winter and Strober collections in Germany. He received the Fine Arts National Prize in 1998.

Ernesto García Peña (Matanzas, 1949). Painter, engraver and professor. He has a rich teaching career in the specialties of drawing, engraving and painting. He has more than fifty personal and collective exhibitions. Since 1970, he is a collaborator in several books and journals of several publishing houses. He has large format stained glass murals and paintings on ceramic pieces for several Cuban institutions. He received the First Prize in the Mariana Grajales Competition, 1984; Painting Mention, UNEAC Salon, 1985; in 1994, Only Mention in Drawing, Abanico Salon, Havana and in 1996 he received the National Cultura Distinction.

Miguel Mejides (Camagüey, 1950). Narrator. He has published several books among which are: *Tiempo de hombres* (short store, 1977); *El jardín de las flores silvestres* (UNEAC Prize, short story, 1983); *Rumba Palace* (story, 1995), and *Perversiones en El Prado* (novel,1999). He won the Juan Rulfo Prize of Radio France International in 1995.

GO ON BEING ME /35

Aymara Aymerich Carrasco (Havana, 1976). Poet and narrator. Some of the books she has published are: *in útero* (poetry, 2000), *Deseos líquidos* (short story, 2000) and *Cuerpo sobre cuerpo sobre cuerpo* (poetry, 2000). She obtained the Calendario Prize in short stories, 1998. In poetry, she was awarded the David Prize in 1999, and the Nosside Caribe, 2001, among others.

Alicia Leal Veloz (Sancti Spíritus, 1957). Painter, engraver, ceramist. Member of IAFA. She has participated in more than ninety personal and collective exhibitions. Her works can be found in permanent collections in the United States, Germany, Jamaica and Nicaragua among others. She obtained the Third Prize in the Salón Paisaje´90 prize and in 2001 she received the National Cultura Distinction.

Eduardo M. Abela Torrás (Havana, 1963). Painter and engraver. He has participated in more than forty personal and collective exhibitions. He received the Engraving Prize in the XVIII Salon, 13 de Marzo Competition, Cuba and in 2000, he received the Special Prize and Prize of the Visual Arts Development Center, 2nd International Biennial of DDT.

Alexis Díaz-Pimienta (Havana, 1966). Narrator, poet, researcher and repentist (improviser). Among his publications are: *Huitzel y Quetzal* (Luis Rogelio Nogueras Short Store Prize, 1991); *Los visitantes del sábado* (short store, 1994); *En Almería casi nunca llueve* (Surco de Poesía, Seville International Prize, 1996); *Teoría de la improvisación* (research, 1998), and *Prisionero del agua* (novel, Alba / Prensa Canaria Prize, 1998). He has received the National Cultura Distinction.

Emilio Comas Paret (Caibarién, 1942). Poet and narrator. He has Publisher a collection of poems, a book of short stories and two novels. He obtained mentions in the David, 1973 competition, La *Gaceta de Cuba,* short store, 1997, and Casa de Teatro, the Dominican Republic, 2001, with his novel *El dulce amargo de la desesperación,* among other awards.

Flora Fong (Camagüey, 1949). She works in painting, sculpture, ceramics, engraving, fabric designer and stained glass. She is a member of the International Association of Fine Arts (IAFA). She has more than one hundred forty personal and collective exhibitions in Cuba and abroad. She has received the following distinctions: First Prize in Drawing, National Salon of professors, 1975; Mention in Painting, Carlos Enriquez National Salon, 1980, and IAFA Prize, UNEAC salon, 1985. She was awarded the Distinction of Illustrious Daughter of the city of Camagüey and of National Culture.

Antonio Vidal (Havana, 1928). Painter, sculptor and engraver. He has had more than ninety personal and collective exhibitions around the world. He has made medium and large format murals, textile designs and illustrations for books and journals. His work enriches permanent collections in museums and galleries nationally and abroad. He has been recognized with the National Prize of Fine Arts, 1999; the Alejo Carpentier Medal, 1994and the Order Félix Varela, 1st degree, 2002.

Aida Bahr (Holguín, 1958). Narrator and script writer. Among her work published are: *Ellas, de noche* (short story, 1989); *Rafael Soler, una mirada al hombre* (essay, 1995), and *Espejismos* (short story,1998). Some of her work has been included in anthologies such as *El submarino amarillo* and *Estatuas de sal.*

David Mitrani Arenal (Havana, 1966). Poet and narrator. He has Publisher the following books: *Modelar el barro* (short story, 1993), *Santos lugares* (short story, 1997) and *Ganeden* (novel, Mexico, 1999). Among his distinctions are: the Cucalambé de Décima National Prize, 1993; the La Rambla Poetry Prize, Spain, 1995, and the Anna Seghers Prize for his work awarded by the Foundation of the same name, Berlín, 1998.

Juan Moreira (Havana, 1938). Painter, lithographer and engraver. He is a member of IAFA and has had more than seventy personal and collective exhibitions. Some of his work is part of permanent collections of Schools Museum, Gotha, Germany; National Museum, Szceczin, Poland; Museum of the Americas, Managua, Nicaragua; Royal Ontario Museum, Canada and the Cuban National Museum of Fine Arts. Among other awards he obtained the First Prize in Drawing, professor' Salon , 1973, and Honor Mention in the 7th Painting Biennial, Kosice, Czechoslovakia, in 1984. In 1988, he received the National Culture Distinction.

THE GHOSTS  **/97**

Mylene Fernández Pintado (Pinar del Río, 1963). Lawyer and narrator. She has published *Anhedonia* (David Prize, short story, 1998). She has received two mentions in the La *Gaceta de Cuba* Competition as well as in the Fernando González International Competition in Colombia, and the Prize for Novels in the Italo Calvino Competition (2002) with her work *Otras plegarias atendidas.*

Adigio Benítez Jimeno (Santiago de Cuba, 1924). Painter, poet, professor. He has participated in many personal and collective exhibitions. His work can be found in the Collection of Cuban Art in the National Museum of Fine Arts and in private collections in Cuba and abroad. His distinctions include the Painting Prize of the National Salon, 1961, Drawing Prize of the National Salon, 1962; Mention II Triennial of Realism, Bulgaria, 1976; the René Portocarrero First Prize and Grand Prize, UNEAC Salon, 1985; the Félix Varela Order, 1st degree in 1994, and the National Fine Arts Prize, 2002.

BETINA'S MONOLOG **/107**

Marilyn Bobes (Havana, 1955). Poet, narrator, literary critic and editor. She obtained the David Prize in poetry, 1979, with *La aguja en el pajar.* She has also published collections of poems such as *Hallar el modo* (1989); *Revi(c)itaciones* and *Homenajes* (1998). In 1993 she obtained the Edmundo Valadés Latina American Short Story Prize in Mexico and in 1994 she obtained the Magda Portal Women's Prize of Hispanic–American Short Stories in Peru. In 1995, she was awarded the Casa de las Américas Prize with her book of short stories, *Alguien tiene que llorar* (1996).

Rafael Morante (Madrid, 1931). Graphic designer, illustrator, painter, professor, cartoonist, fantastic literatura writer. (David Prize of science fiction, UNEAC, 1984). He has received many distinctions that include: the National Cultura Distinction; the Space Prize, 2001 for his *La Obra de la Vida*, of the National Association of Publicists and Propagandists of Cuba; and the National Prize for Book Design. 2001.

Rafael Zarza González (Havana, 1944). Painter and lithographer. He has participated in more than three hundred personal and collective exhibitions in several Countries. His work is found in national and international museums, private collections. Since 1965, he is a member of the Experimental Graphics Workshop of Havana. He has obtained several awards such as: the Portinari Lithography Prize, Casa de las Américas, 1968; the Special Prize, XXV Anniversary of the Revolution, UNEAC Salon, 1984, and the Prize in the Arte en la Carretera Competition, 1985.

Enrique Núñez Rodríguez (Quemado de Güines, 1923-Havana, 2002). Journalist and narrator. Among his work Publisher are: *Sube, Felipe, sube* (1980); *Yo vendí mi bicicleta* (1989); *Oye, cómo lo cogieron* (1991); *Gente que yo quise* (1995), and *Mi vida al desnudo* (2000).Among the many awards received are: the National Cultura Distinction, 1981; the José Martí National Prize of Journalism, 1989; the Félix Varela Order, 1st degree, 1992; the National Prize of Humor, 2001, and the National Prize of Radio, 2002.

Juan Carlos Rodriguéz (Havana, 1943). Researcher and narrator. Among his books Publisher are: *Ellos merecen la victoria* (26 de Julio, 1981 Testimony Prize); *El último retorno* (Prize for Novels, MININT, 1991); *Vuelo 455* (26 de Julio, Novel Prize,1993), and *La batalla inevitable* (testimony, 1996).

Carlos Montes de Oca (Camagüey, 1968). Self taught painter. His work has been presented in more than forty personal and collective exhibitions, in Cuba and abroad. He received the 13 de Marzo Competition Painting Prize, Havana University, 1991 y 1993.

Eduardo Roca Salazar, Choco (Santiago de Cuba, 1949). Painter and engraver. He is a member of IAFA. He has had many personal and collective exhibitions. Among his professional activities are as Chair of Painting in the San Alejandro Fine Arts Academy and Collage Courses in the Pilar and Joan Miro Foundation, Spain, in 1994, and in San Francisco, United States in 2001. He has permanent exhibits in the Africa Museum, Chicago; Museo de la Estampa, Mexico; the Ludwig Foundation, Germany; the Museums of Yokohama and Kochi, Japan, among others. He obtained the First Prize in small format engraving in the Orense Competition, Spain, 1984 and the Grand Prize of the IV International Triennial of Engraving, Kochi, Japan, 1999.

Alberto Guerra Naranjo (Havana, 1963). Narrator and professor. Among his publications are: *Disparos en El aula* (short story, 1994); *Aporías de la feria* (short story, 1996), and *Blasfemia del escriba* (short story, 2001). He has been awarded the Luis Rogelio Nogueras Prize, 1992; the Short Store Prize of *La Gaceta de Cuba,* 1997 and 1999, and the Ernest Hemingway Short Story Prize, 1998.

THE DAUGHTER OF DARIO /157

Adelaida Fernández de Juan (Havana, 1961). Physician and narrator. Among her publications are: *Dolly y otros cuentos africanos* (1994); *Clemencia bajo el sol* (Grand Prize Cecilia Valdés, 1996), and *Oh vida* (UNEAC Prize, short story, 1998).

Zaida del Río (Villa Clara, 1954). Draftswoman, engraver, decorator of ceramics and illustrator. She has had many personal and collective exhibitions. In 1984, she received the Lithography Prize, National Graphics Conference, Cuba; in 1993 she received the Gold Medal, First Prize in the Painting Biennial in Cairo, Egypt and the Painting Prize in the Tenri Biennial, Japan, in 1998.

THE PHOENIX /165

Jesús David Curbelo (Camagüey, 1965). Poet, narrator, critic. Included in his publications are: *Diario de un poeta recién cazado* (novel, 1999); *Tres tristes triángulos* (short story, 2000); *El lobo y el centauro* (poetry, 2001), y *Cirios* (poetry, 2002). He has received the following distinctions; the David Prize for Poetry, 1991; the José Soler Puig Prize for Novel, 1998; the Distinction of National Culture, 1999, and the Oriente Prize for Short Story, 2002, among others.

Manuel Mendive Hoyo (Havana, 1944). Painter and sculptor. He has participated in more than ninety personal and collective exhibitions in national and international scenarios. He has a large volume of work in performances. He has obtained the Adam Montparnasse Prize in the XXIV May Salon, France, in 1968; the International Prize in the II Biennial of Havana in 1986; the Félix Varela Order, 1st degree and was granted Knight of the Order of Arts and Literature of the Francophone Culture, Ministry of the French Republic, 1994, and the National Prize of Fine Arts, 2001.

THE NIGHT OF THE GHOSTS /171

Rogelio Riverón (Placetas, 1964). Narrator, poet and journalist. Some of his publications are the following: *Los equivocados* (Luis Rogelio Nogueras Prize, short story, 1990); *Subir al cielo y otras equivocaciones* (Pinos Nuevos Prize, short story, 1995); *Buenos días, Zenón* (UNEAC Prize, short store, 1999), and *Otras versiones del miedo* (UNEAC Prize, short story, 2001). In 1997 he received the National Cultural Journalism Prize and Mention in the Casa de las Americas Prize in 2001.

José Omar Torres López (Matanzas, 1953). Painter, lithographer, engraver and professor. He has more than a hundred personal and collective exhibitions. He has given engraving courses in Colombia, Ecuador, Sweden and Norway. Much of his work is in collections of the Fine Arts National Museum; Schrainer Museum in Cologne, Germany; Fenix Foundation of Stockholm, Sweden; Workshop Brandywine, Philadelphia, United States, among others. Currently he is directing the Experimental Workshop of Graphics.

Edel Bordón (Las Villas, 1953). Painter and professor. His work has been represented in several personal and collective exhibitions in Cuba and abroad. For his vast work as a teacher, he has received many distinctions such as: Mention for Pedagogy, National Center pf Art Education and Prize for the Pedagogic Masters, Havana University, 1996 and 1998.

Daniel Chavarría (Cuban writer born in Uruguay, 1933). Narrator, script writer for films and TV, professor, translator. Among his novels the most important are: *Joy* (1978, MININT Prize for the best Cuban detective novel of the 70s); *Allá ellos* (Premio *Dashiell Hammett* Prize of AIEP in Gijón, Asturias, 1992), *El ojo de Cibeles* (Planeta Prize, Mexico, 1993); *El rojo en la pluma del loro* (Casa de las Américas Prize, 2000), and *Adiós muchachos* (E. Allan Poe Prize, New York, 2002).

Ernesto M. Rancaño Vieites (Havana, 1968). Painter and draftsman. He is a member of IAFA and has more than fifty personal and collective exhibitions. Some of his work decorates tourist installations in the country. He is coauthor of the art book entitled *Suceden los espejos.*

Marta Rojas Rodríguez (Santiago de Cuba, 1931). Narrator and journalist. Included among her works are: *El juicio del Moncada,* testimony published for the first time in 1960; *Crónicas sobre Viet Nam* (of the South and the North, 1966 and 1971); *El que debe vivir* (Casa de las Américas Prize for testimony, 1978); *El columpio de Rey Spencer* (novel, 1996); *Santa lujuria* (novel, 2000). She obtained the José Martí National Journalism Prize in 1998.

Ricardo Alarcón de Quesada (Havana, 1937). Doctor in Philosophy and Arts in Havana University. Of his rich political life, noteworthy is his participation as member of the Provincial Direction of the 26th of July Movement in Havana (1957-1959), President of the University Federation of Students (1961-1962) and member of the Political Bureau of the Cuban Communist Party since 1992. He has occupied different posts in the government such as the Director for Latin America of the Foreign Affairs Ministry, Permanent ambassador of Cuba to the United Nations, President of the Administrative Council of the UNDP, Vice Minister and Minister of Foreign Affairs and President of the National Assembly of Popular Power since 1993.